THE HUNGRY TIGRESS

The Hungry Tigress

AND OTHER TRADITIONAL ASIAN TALES

Told by Rafe Martin

Illustrated by Richard Wehrman

SHAMBHALA
Boulder & London   1984

SHAMBHALA PUBLICATIONS, INC.

Box 271
Boulder, Colorado 80306

© 1984 by Rafe Martin
All rights reserved
9 8 7 6 5 4 3 2 1
First Edition
Distributed in the United States by Random House
and in Canada by Random House of Canada Ltd.
Distributed in the United Kingdom by Routledge & Kegan Paul Ltd.,
London and Henley-on-Thames.
Printed in the United States of America.

Library of Congress Cataloging in Publication Data
Martin, Rafe, 1946-
  The hungry tigress and other traditional Asian tales.
  1. Tipitaka. Suttapitaka. Khuuddakanikāya. Jātaka—
Paraphrases, English. I. Tipitaka. Suttapitaka.
Khuddakanikāya. Jātaka. II. Title.
BQ1462.E5M37   1984   294.3'823   83-20278
ISBN 0-87773-275-2
ISBN 0-87773-261-2 (pbk.)
ISBN 0-394-53698-3 (Random House)
ISBN 0-394-72339-2 (pbk.: Random House)

Design/Eje Wray
Chapter illustration/Gail Renlund
Typesetting/Linotron Trump/The Type Galley
Printing/McNaughton & Gunn
Cover design & illustration/Richard Wehrman

CONTENTS

INTRODUCTION

Most of the stories in this collection of traditional Asian tales are Jatakas, that is, tales of the Buddha's earlier births. Jataka tales are perhaps the most persistently popular and widespread of all traditional Asian stories. They have been told, drawn, painted, and performed in literally every Asian country and kingdom. References to them can be traced back almost 2500 hundred years, to just about the time of the historical Buddha.

Carvings on sacred shrines in India, depicting scenes from the Jatakas, clearly indicate that Jatakas were well-known, indeed, already quite popular, in the third century B.C. Many of the tales are, however, considerably older. So, while they may have been originally told by the Buddha himself—as tradition asserts—it is also likely that some were told by later generations of Buddhist teachers and storytellers who, finding a teaching of interest or significance in a yet more ancient tale, reworked and retold it as a "jataka" or "birthlet." This endless process of change, transformation, and recreation is, after all, at the very heart of the oral tradition. It has been going on for many thousands of years, all around the world.

However, the Jatakas are not only some of the oldest stories in the world, they are also some of the most popular. They exist in countless variants throughout Asia and have been cited as a major source for both *Aesop's Fables* and the

Arabian Nights. The Jatakas reached Europe in the Middle Ages where they influenced the works of Chaucer, Spenser, Shakespeare, and, later, to come full circle in our own time, *The Jungle Books* of Rudyard Kipling. They also entered the popular culture in the form of numerous folk tales and rhymes long known in the West in many variant forms. (To mention just two—both the Tar-Baby story and the tale of Chicken Little, or "The Sky is Falling," go back to the Jatakas. The "originals" are included in this collection as, respectively, "Prince Five-Weapons" and "The Brave Lion and the Foolish Little Rabbit.") So the Jatakas have already had a long and varied history in the West.

Some 550 of these "birth-stories" were recorded in the Pali in the fifth century A.D. This vast collection, titled simply *The Jataka*, contains an amazingly wide range of stories—sensitive animal fables, monkish moralizings, inspiring heroic epics; in short, fragments of many different elements of the culture. It has been called by one early Western commentator, "the oldest, most complete and most important collection of folk-lore extant." All the stories in it, however, are held together by a simple thread: all are purported to have been told by the Buddha himself. And all, no matter what their subject, are to be seen as presenting his earlier births—whether as animal, man, god, or spirit. The entire collection, too, is actually only a fragment of a much older and vaster epic and oral tradition which has been lost to us.

Through somewhat later Sanskrit collections, like *The Jatakamala*, or *Garland of Jatakas*, by Aryasura—one of the most famous Jataka collections of all—the tales took on their characteristic vision. In these works tales that emphasize compassion and self-sacrifice were given preeminence. Even today such tales are recognized as the keys to the tradition. Through them, the Jatakas became a celebration of a life of noble deeds.

In *The Hungry Tigress* I have aimed at restoring, from both Pali and Sanskrit sources, some of these dramatic, lively, and often moving traditional Asian tales for modern Western audiences.

As in actual oral telling, the stories in this collection run a range from the gentle, humorous tales which establish and define values—what we have come to think of today as "children's stories"—to powerful testing tales which show these values being tested, often bitterly, in life.

Traditional cultures wisely refrain from separating literature into what we call "juvenile" and "adult." Good stories and live storytelling have, and I suppose always will have, equal appeal to both adults and children. After all, such questions as, What is good?, What is evil?, What were things like long ago?, What is the right way to live?, have no sharply defined age limits.

So this book, like a traditional storytelling, is for both adults and children. It is something to be shared. Some tales may, of course, appeal more to children. Others will seem more serious, reflective, and "adult." But, again, we should keep in mind that traditional tales were never intended for the nursery. They existed for the whole community, adults and children, and were meant to awaken and restore that community to the values on which its society was based. They did this by demonstrating those values in life, in action; not by philosophizing about them. Whether formally told at religious festivals or informally presented while seated around a fire, the common language of story is wonder and delight. Storytelling is a participatory experience drawing on deep feelings and calling forth strong emotions—from humor and fear to exaltation, pity, and tears.

As a storyteller, I am fascinated by these traditional Asian tales. Their range is immense; their commitment to compassion, the highest of all virtues, often astonishing. Respect and love for all living things, courage, perseverance, good humor and faith: these are the Jatakas' universal "message." And it is one that all of us—East and West, adult and child—can, I think, stand to hear again.

The last story in the book, "Stillson's Leap," I should point out, is, unlike all the others, not a traditional tale. Rather, after performing the Jatakas as a storyteller so many times and after working on these modern, oral-like versions, I couldn't resist trying to create a modern Jataka, one that would express the tradition in our own terms and time.

The other stories are all my own recreations of traditional Asian tales which extend back several thousand years at the very least. However, three tales, "The Arising of Bodhi," "Leaving Home," and "Enlightenment," while quite famous and quite traditional Asian stories, are not, technically speaking, Jatakas. Rather, they form part of the larger context in terms of which the Jataka tales would have been traditionally viewed. As such, they cease being simply tales and come closer to our own conception of myth.

Any Asian audience would, of course, bring knowledge of the events of the Buddha's life—as well as knowledge of other Jataka tales—with them to the experience of any single birth-story. In fact, a long history of the Buddha's past births—going back hundreds of thousands of millenia and into previous world cycles—as well as the events of his last existence up until the attainment of enlightenment, actually form the Introduction to the Pali Jataka. As with the Arthurian cycles in the West, these stories are to be seen as forming a single, large, imaginative, and spiritual structure. And it is in terms of this entire body of story that any single and seemingly simple tale takes on its deeper, more resonant life.

Traditional tales in every culture, then, are only one element of the complex of shared feelings and understandings common to all the members of the society. They are a

small, visible portion of the common inner ground. So, their significance is very great.

The Jatakas, too, of course, embody much of the richness of their Indian and, specifically, Buddhist heritage. Magical transformations occur. Time is measured on a grand, incalculably vast, cosmic scale. The reality of countless past, and future, lifetimes is tacitly assumed. One hears of other worlds and realms. One may encounter other kinds of beings. All living things communicate, have moral and spiritual struggles, as well as the potential for courage, goodness, wisdom. All creatures seem to spring from a common ground. And all are judged according to similar standards. What's more, there is a deep yearning for, and faith in, the ultimate, ongoing, higher evolution of all life. In short, in these tales one enters an indescribably ancient, vast, multi-leveled, highly moral universe. A universe which, while acknowledging pain and suffering, expresses both a deep commitment to compassion and an all-pervasive respect for every living thing.

However, *The Hungry Tigress* is a collection of stories, not a philosophy. As such, it is, after all, like all storytelling, meant to entertain as much as to instruct. I hope, then, that you will enjoy these new versions of some of the traditional Jataka tales. They are authentic tellings set, once again, in their traditional contexts. I dedicate them to everyone who likes stories—young and old, in all times, everywhere.

R.M.
Rochester
June, 1983

The Arising
of Bodhi

Once,
long ago,

when this world was very young, or in another world, the Buddha was born as a mighty prince. Now this prince always expected his servants and attendants to give their absolute best to any task he might set for them. He would take no excuses for anything less than perfection and excellence.

Yet he was fair in his own way, too. He expected himself to maintain the same high standards that he set for others.

One day the prince called for his elephant trainer and told him to prepare the mighty white elephant to carry him to the mango groves.

"Sir," replied the elephant trainer, "the great white elephant has burst from the stalls and reentered the jungle. The season of rut is upon him and he could not be held."

"What!" cried the mighty prince in a sudden rage. "What kind of training is this? What sort of elephant trainer are you, who cannot control your beasts?"

"But Noble Prince, he will return!" exclaimed the elephant keeper. "The discipline was good. Though he may roam far, the bonds of his training are strong; they cannot be broken. You shall see, Lord. He will be back soon."

But the prince was not satisfied. Angry still, he struck the elephant keeper a blow with his palm and dismissed him in disgust.

The next day the elephant keeper returned, proudly leading the great elephant who, though red-eyed and caked with mud, had returned on his own, just as the trainer had predicted. "You see, my prince," announced the keeper, patting the great beast upon the thick, wrinkled skin of his swaying trunk, "it is as I said, is it not? He knows his master. We have indeed conquered his old, wild ways."

With those words the prince awoke as if from a dream. He had been brooding over his own loss of control. "Conquered?" he now exclaimed. "Trainer, tell me," he went on, "do you know of any who have truly conquered themselves; who are never pulled away from what is right, and so, need never struggle to return?"

"Yes," said the trainer, as if remembering something long forgotten. "Yes, there are the Conquerors, the Awakened Ones of old. They have attained the Truth and will never strike out blindly again. But with firm will and compassionate hearts, they now boldly walk the Way."

Then a yearning arose in the prince's heart, a sudden, wild, unconquerable yearning to attain the Truth and conquer himself at last.

It is said that this was the first time the Buddha of our age, as an ordinary man, long ago, actually awoke to a yearning for the Way. Much hardship and effort and many trials still lay ahead. But, as you shall see, he was successful.

The Brave Lion and the Foolish Rabbit

Once

there was

a foolish little rabbit. One day this little rabbit was resting quietly beneath a tree. He wasn't fully awake, but he wasn't completely asleep either. He was just drifting between waking and sleeping. As he lay there with the green, leafy branches swaying above him, and the white clouds drifting slowly overhead, a foolish thought filled his mind. "What if the earth broke up?" he thought. Suddenly he heard a loud CRASH! just behind him.

Up jumped the little rabbit yelling, "Oh my gosh! Oh my gosh! The earth is breaking up! It is breaking up!"

And, without looking around, he started running as fast as he could, yelling, "The earth's breaking up! The earth's breaking up!" as he went.

As he ran he passed another rabbit. And that rabbit said to him, "Say, friend, where are you going? What's the big hurry? Hey, stop! Slow down! What's going on?"

But the foolish rabbit wouldn't stop; he wouldn't slow down. He was too scared. He just kept running, and as he ran, he shouted back, "The earth's breaking up! The earth's breaking up! Get going! Get going!"

When the other rabbit heard the news he got scared and started running, too. Both rabbits ran together shouting, "The earth's breaking up! The earth's breaking up! Get going! Get going!" as loud as they could.

Pretty soon they passed a third rabbit. "Say, friends," he called out, "where are you going? Why are you running? What's happening? What's up?" But the first two rabbits were too scared to stop and explain. They just kept running. As they ran, though, they shouted back, "The earth's breaking up! Get going! Get going!" Well, when the third rabbit heard that, he got scared and he started running too.

The three rabbits ran on together. They passed another rabbit and another. Soon there were five rabbits, then ten rabbits, then twenty rabbits, then thirty rabbits, then fifty rabbits, then one hundred rabbits, all hopping and leaping along as fast as their legs could carry them. And all were shouting, "The earth's breaking up! The earth's breaking up! Get going! Get going!" at the top of their lungs.

All these rabbits ran past a big, sleepy bear. And the bear rubbed his sleepy eyes and said slowly, "Wha-at's happen-ing? Why are you all run-ning? Hey, stop! Where are you go-ing? What do you mean, 'The earth's breaking up?'" But the rabbits were too scared. They wouldn't stop. They just kept running. And as they ran they shouted out, "The earth's breaking up!" Naturally, the bear got scared. "The earth's break-ing up? The earth's break-ing up?" he thought in dismay. "Why, if the earth's break-ing up, I'd better get going, too!" And he started running. Now a bear can't move like a rabbit, but still, all in all, he was barreling along at a good pace. And, as he ran, he called out in his slow, sturdy, bear's voice, "Earth's break-ing up! Earth's break-ing up! Get go-ing! Get go-ing!"

Pretty soon, he ran past another bear. "Where are you going?" that bear called out to him. "Why are you running? Hey stop! Slow down! What's going on?" But the first bear wouldn't stop. He wouldn't slow down. He was too scared. As he ran, he just called out over his shoulder, "The earth's breaking up! Earth's breaking up! Get going! Get going!"

Well, when the second bear heard that, he got scared,

too, and he started running. Soon both these bears ran past a third bear. He was sitting quietly on the ground, chewing on a fresh piece of dripping honeycomb and batting slowly at the bees which circled, buzzing angrily, all around him. "Hey!" he said. "Why are you running? What's going on?" But the two bears were too scared to stop—they were too scared to even ask for some of that sweet honeycomb. They just ran right past. But as they ran, they called out together, "The earth's breaking up! Get going!"

"What! What's that you say?" said the third bear rising to his feet. "The earth's breaking up? The earth's breaking up? Hey, wait for me!" And pushing all of the honeycomb into his mouth he scrambled off, leaving the puzzled bees circling in the empty air. "Earth's breaking up?" they buzzed. "Let's beat it!" And they too flew off, in a long wavering column, behind the three terrified bears.

Pretty soon they all ran past another bear and another. Before long there were five bears running, then ten bears, then twenty bears, then thirty bears, then fifty bears, then one hundred bears all barreling along as fast as they could. As they ran, they were all shouting, "The earth's breaking up! The earth's breaking up! Get going! Get going!" Oh, what a howling and growling; what a horrible, mournful din they made!

As all these bears ran through the jungle, they came upon an elephant. He was standing under a great shade tree, resting, half-asleep. His eyes were closed. His huge ears fanned slowly back and forth. His tail swished this way and that, sweeping off the droning flies. Suddenly his ears fanned forward and stopped. His eyes opened wide. Thumping and shouting and screaming and yelling, a crowd of wide-eyed bears went tearing past.

"Say!" he trumpeted, lifting up his snakelike trunk, "What's going on! What's happening? Why are you all running?"

And the bears, without slowing down a bit, shouted back, "It's the earth! The earth! It's breaking up! Run! Run!"

When the elephant heard that, he was wide awake at once. "Why," he said, "I'm the biggest and the heaviest of all creatures. If the earth's breaking up, I'd be the first one to fall in! I'd better get going!" And, trumpeting wildly, he too charged off, his tail pointed straight out behind him. The astonished flies buzzed on, rising and falling around the spot that the frightened elephant had just left. And then they too set out, glittering and circling after the terrified elephant as fast as they could.

The elephant charged along, tearing through the jungle, tossing aside branches and even whole trees as he went. Huge clouds of dust rose up around him and with his trunk he poured more red dust on his domed head as he ran. "Woe! Woe!" he trumpeted in sadness and terror. "The earth, the earth, my dear, dear earth is breaking up!"

He, of course, soon ran past another elephant and pretty soon there were two, then three, then five elephants running madly. In fact, to make a long story short, there were soon one hundred huge, terrified elephants stampeding through the jungle and over the plains, tearing up bushes and trees, making so much noise that it was deafening and raising so much dust that it became hard to see the bright, golden sun!

Now all these elephants, in their terror, ran right past a snake. The snake, of course, had heard and felt them coming for some time. His hole had begun to shake. Bits and pieces of his ceiling had begun dropping upon him. He woke up. He opened one eye. He opened the other. "Whatsss happening?" he thought. "Isss it an earthquake?" Pretty soon he was bouncing around so much that he was getting bruised just lying there! He raised his smooth head and slid out of his den, flicking his pink tongue before him—just in time to see the herd of frightened elephants storming past.

"Sssay brothersss," he hissed, "what isss going on here? What'sss happening?"

And the elephants screamed madly, "The earth's breaking up! That's what's happening! Get going! Get going!"

Well, when the snake heard that, he said to himself, "If the earthsss breaking up, it'sss the end for me. I'd better get sssliding." And wasting no time, he began to slide quickly along the ground. He slid over boulders and stones; he slid around trees and stumps; he slid under bushes and logs. Soon he slid past another snake.

"Ssssay," said that snake, "what'sss the hurry?"

But the first snake just hissed, "Earth'sss breaking up!" and without pausing even for an instant, or diverting the set of his ruby eyes, he flowed quickly over stones and stumps and was gone!

Naturally enough, the word got around. In a very short time, there were three, then five, then ten, then twenty, then thirty, then fifty, then one hundred hissing snakes all sliding quickly along over boulders and around stumps. There were one hundred trumpeting elephants tearing along, tossing up bushes and branches and huge clouds of dust. There were one hundred moaning bears, barreling along through the underbrush, and one hundred terrified rabbits, hopping and leaping and bouncing along—not to mention the many flying insects who followed them! And all, all were shouting at the top of their panting lungs, "The earth is breaking up! The earth is breaking up! Get going! Get going!"

Now, up on top of a mountain, overlooking this jungle, there was a brave lion, asleep. He heard all the shouting and noise, and opening his golden eyes, looked out over the jungles and plains. There, below him, he saw all the animals running, running, running madly as if pursued by some terrible danger. Looking carefully, he saw nothing at all threatening them. But he did see that they were running straight toward the edge of a cliff. And he saw that if no one stopped them, they would fall over the edge of that cliff and die.

"Someone should help those animals," he said quietly to himself, rising to his feet.

"Why, I'll help them," he decided. Gathering all his strength, he took a tremendous lion LEAP! way out over the jungle. With his mane streaming behind him, he landed, roaring, in front of all the terrified animals. When the animals found the lion standing before them, sounding his deep and mighty lion's roar, when they saw his tail twitching from side to side and his great paws and teeth blocking the path, they all came screeching to a halt.

"Why are you all running?" roared the lion.

"Because the earth's breaking up! The earth's breaking up!" screamed the animals together. "Oh, please, let us through, mighty lion! Don't block our path! Oh, please, get going! Get going, before we are all killed!"

"Raahrrr!" roared the lion. "Look, you silly creatures," he said. "The earth isn't breaking up. It's not breaking up at all." He struck the earth a powerful blow with his paw. "Here's the earth! Solid as it's ever been. Who told you that the earth was breaking up?"

"Elephants!" hissed the snakes.

"Bears!" trumpeted the elephants.

"Rabbits!" growled the bears.

"Him!" said the rabbits pointing at each other. "Him!" "Him!" "Him!" "No him!" they said, going back and forth until they finally traced it all the way back to one tiny, terrified rabbit who stood there shaking and stammering in his fright. "Ye-es, I said it. The earth is breaking up! I heard it with my own ears! Oh, get going! Get going! Please get going! Oh, run! Run!"

"Wait!" said the lion. Then, turning to the little rab-

bit, he asked in a kindly voice, "Where did you say you heard this earth breaking up?"

"Back there. By my tree," quaked the little rabbit.

"Well," said the lion, "let's go back and see what it was that you heard and thought was the sound of the earth breaking up." But the little rabbit was too scared. "No!" he said, "Uh-uh! I'm not going back to that tree! Not on your life! I just won't!"

The lion opened his jaws wide and roared, "Raahrrr!"

Then the rabbit said, "Okay! Okay! I'll go!"

So the lion said, "Get on my back." And the rabbit did. Then the lion took one! two! three! tremendous lion leaps and landed all the way back at the tree. There it was, still growing quietly in the heart of the forest, just where the rabbit had left it. The lion stalked all around the tree sniffing the earth. He reached down with his paw and lifted something so the rabbit could see. "Here's your earth breaking up, you foolish little rabbit," he laughed. "Here's the source of the noise you heard!"

And do you know what it was? Why, it was an apple! Just an apple! The rabbit's ears drooped and his face got very red. He took a deep breath and hung his head. "Oh," he said in a very small voice, "so that was what I heard? Oh my, it's very embarrassing. What a mistake! What a fuss over nothing! But anybody could have thought the sound of an apple falling was the sound of the earth breaking up—couldn't they?"

"No!" laughed the lion again. "You are a foolish little rabbit, after all. Let's go back and tell the others." Then, taking one! two! three! tremendous lion leaps, he returned to where all the animals were waiting. "Go ahead," he said, "tell them."

The little rabbit took a deep breath. "Well, you see, I didn't really hear the earth breaking up after all. It was just this apple I heard, when it fell to the ground. Uh, you can understand that, um, can't you?"

But the animals couldn't understand it. They shouted "No!" and were so upset that they wanted to tear that little rabbit to pieces.

But the lion said, "Wait! Remember, you all ran, too. Why not take this as a lesson. Next time something frightens you, face it. Find out what the fuss is all about. Once you've faced it for yourselves, perhaps you'll discover that it too, like this apple that fell in the forest, is really nothing to be scared of at all."

All the animals said, "Why, next time we'll do that!" Then they went back to their homes.

The brave lion took a tremendous LEAP!, waaay up, back onto his mountaintop. He lay down, yawned once, closed his eyes, and was soon fast asleep again.

And the little rabbit, still holding the apple, hopped back to his tree. He lay down under it. Once again he watched the green branches swaying and the white clouds drifting high overhead. He sighed peacefully. Content at last, he took a big BITE out of the apple!

The Steadfast Parrot and his Tree

Once
there was

a parrot. His feathers were green, red, and yellow. His sharp, curved beak was yellow, too, and he had golden circles around his black, shining eyes.

This parrot lived in a fig tree. He loved the tree. He loved it for the shade it cast over him and for the way the harsh sunlight softened as it fell through the green, glowing leaves. He loved the tree also for its sweet fruit and for its swaying branches. He loved all its whisperings, its endless creakings and rustlings which, to him, sounded, in the wind at night like a sweet, unearthly music. During the hot days, he loved the feel of the cool, smooth bark beneath his toes. The tree was his home and the center of his world.

Every evening as he flew back over the forest and perched among the softly fluttering leaves he thought, "How happy I am living in this tree. How content I am, how peaceful and free here. I owe my tree so much. I'll never abandon my tree, my home, for any other refuge."

Now, in this world there live more than just the men, women, children, plants, and animals that we see. Gods, demons, imps, and spirits share this living earth with us; some are above us in wisdom and power, some equal to us, and some below. Every word we speak echoes in some other world.

The high god, Shakra himself, heard the parrot and decided to test him. Raising his arm, he blasted the tree and withered and dried it until the leaves blackened and died. Dust lay on the branches where the sweet dew used to collect.

But the parrot would not leave. He sat on the bare, dead branches, eating dust. Slowly lifting his claws, he climbed from branch to branch, circling the tree to keep from the glaring sunlight which beat upon him. He stayed with his tree. In his heart he could see it, covered not with dust, but with bright leaves, still swaying and rustling in the afternoon breeze. "What?" he thought to himself. "Should friends part just because bitter fortune has struck? Days pass and fortunes change. My words were sincere and true/And my tree I'll not leave you."

Days passed. Still the parrot remained hopeful and content. Perched on the dead branches among the dry, rattling leaves, eating the dust and sheltering only with difficulty from the heat of the sun, he did not let his spirit break or yield up his heart of contentment. "Life is change, after all," he said. "And bird or not, the Truth is still the Truth."

The Shakra, smiling, raised his arm. Once again a golden breeze blew. Buds formed, leaves unfolded, fruits swelled, and the dust, whirling, blew suddenly away. Amazed, the parrot sat sheltered once again among the leafy branches of his beloved tree.

"Little bird," said the god, "the whole universe comes to life through a contented heart. Even the lofty gods smile when meeting one who has attained contentment. So, outwardly you may only be a little bird, yet, I commend you. Within, you do indeed bear the precious gift of life. Live contented with your tree/And may all beings so contented be."

Laughing, the god Shakra rose into the bluest of blue skies. And the contented little parrot, once again sipping the sweet dew, rubbed his beak against the cool, smooth bark. Oh, how contented he was!

The Falcon and the Quail

Once,

a little quail

decided that he had had enough of pecking out a living on the hard, sun-baked earth. "I'll make my way into the green fields," he thought to himself. "I need a change."

Flapping his wings, he sailed out over the fields where the tall, green grasses waved in the sunlight. Carried away with delight, he did not notice that a shadow was falling sharply upon him. In less than a minute, he found himself in the clutches of a fierce falcon.

"I'm trapped!" thought the little quail in despair. "What chance do I have!" But then, before fluttering into a final panic, he said to himself, "He is a fierce falcon and I'm just a little quail. Still, if I can just keep my wits about me, I may be able to even the odds yet." And so, instead of weeping and giving himself over to the fear, he now shouted out with all his strength, "Unfair! Unfair!"

The falcon was surprised. No quail had ever responded like this before. Most of them wept and sobbed; some tried pleading with him; a few screamed desperately. He let them. What difference did it make? But never before had he heard such outraged shouts!

And so, instead of carrying the quail directly off to his nest, he began circling on the breeze, still clutching the little bird tightly in his claws. "Why, little bird," he asked, bending his sharp, curved beak, and fierce, yellow eyes down toward the little quail, "whatever do you mean?"

21

"Well," said the quail, trying to keep his heart from thumping wildly, "it hardly seems fair that a powerful hunter like you should have caught me so far from my own home ground. It gives you all the advantage."

"Are you serious?" laughed the falcon, gliding on, but a bit intrigued. To himself he thought, "I'm not all that hungry yet. Why not have a little fun with this loon before eating him?"

"Certainly," said the quail quite boldly now. "No one can catch me when I'm on my own home ground. Not you, and not the biggest bird ever hatched, could catch me when I'm at home!"

"Surely you jest," said the falcon, mildly amused, his powerful beak curving yet more sharply over the defenseless little bird.

"No," said the quail, louder than ever, "why should I jest? If I'm wrong, I'll be your supper anyway. Why?" he added bravely. "Don't you think you can bring it off?"

"Come," said the falcon, irritated despite himself, "show me your field, you foolish little bird. And that," he added with a brief, meaningful squeeze of his claws, "will be that."

When the little quail felt the falcon's claws closing tightly around him, he almost gave up. But then, catching his breath, he called out as loudly as he could, "There it is! Directly below us."

"What," said the falcon, "that bare patch? You must be joking! You can't have grown very strong living there."

"Well," said the quail who had pinned all his hopes on this moment, "just set me down there and we'll soon see who's strongest!"

"All right," said the falcon, "I will!"

And swooping down, he set the little quail free in the very center of the patch. "Be right back," smiled the falcon, and up, up, up he soared, until he was only a tiny dot lost

against the sun. At the top of his climb, he suddenly turned, folded his wings in against his body, and dropped, sharp beak first, straight down, like a living stone, toward the little quail, who sat exposed and alone in the center of the field. Faster and faster and faster he fell.

The defenseless quail watched the falcon growing larger and larger and larger above him; first he seemed to be only a speck, then a dot, then a pebble, then a fierce-eyed bird, talons outstretched, dropping at full speed directly upon him.

At the very last moment, the little quail hopped slightly to one side. And the falcon, wide-eyed, tearing down at his topmost speed, could not stop. CRASH! He hurtled into the rock-hard earth. And that was the end of him.

Then the little quail flapped his wings and trembled all over with relief. He even did a little dance.

And in the future, though he sometimes traveled far from home, he didn't ever again think of flying away from it. After all, on his home ground he was free.

Great Joy, the Self-Respecting Ox

Once
a poor Brahmin

was given an ox-calf. He delighted in the tiny creature. He loved its gentle eyes and awkward, frisky ways. He fed the little ox well and lavished affection and care on it. And the ox loved the man, too. And it grew and grew and GREW! until it was a huge, powerful beast. Yet, big as it was, it was gentle, too. Whatever the Brahmin told it to do, it did—even the heaviest tasks. With good will, it pulled stumps from the fields and dragged boulders. When children wanted a ride, it was willing. So pleased was the Brahmin with the ox that he name it "Great Joy."

One day, Great Joy thought to himself, "The Brahmin, my master, is poor. Yet here am I, a great, powerful ox. I should use my strength to help him. I want to repay all the kindness he has shown."

So Great Joy walked over to the open window of the Brahmin's mud house. Carefully, he put his huge, horned head through the weathered window frame. There sat the Brahmin at a crooked wooden table, mending the torn page of a book. Then the good-hearted ox said, "Dear master, I would like to repay you for the years of kindness you have shown me. I have a plan. Please listen."

Amazed, the Brahmin ceased his work and listened.

"Tomorrow, on the market day," said Great Joy, "when you go into the village, seek out a wealthy merchant. Bet him 1,000 pieces of silver that you have an ox who can pull 100 carts loaded to the top with boulders, gravel, and stone."

"What!" exclaimed the Brahmin, finding his tongue, "I have such an ox?"

"Yes," said Great Joy, "you do. I am that ox."

"Wait, my friend," said the Brahmin. "No ox has ever pulled such a load."

"Trust me," said the ox, "have I ever let you down?"

"No," said the Brahmin upon reflection, "you never have."

"Well, then," continued Great Joy, "don't worry. We'll win the bet. You have my word."

So, in the end, the Brahmin agreed.

The next day, when the sun rose, the poor Brahmin tied on his worn sandals and set off for the town. Entering the already crowded market, he moved through the stalls looking for bargains. He found a piece of white cloth and a few sheets of thick paper, which he bought for a small bag of rice. He also got a fistful of sweet corn for Great Joy.

When the sun rose higher and the day grew very hot, he hurried from the noisy bazaar. He entered a little tea shop where the merchants and farmers gathered to refresh themselves during the midday heat.

He seated himself at a table. Then, gathering his courage, he called out to the wealthy merchant coming through the doorway, "My friend, will you join me?"

"Why not?" said the merchant. Sitting down, he joined the Brahmin at his table.

After pleasantries, a few sweets and some tea, the Brahmin drew a deep breath and announced, "I have an ox."

"So?" responded the wealthy merchant, licking a last crumb of pastry from his fingers. "I have many oxen and, let me tell you, they cost me plenty."

"Yes," said the Brahmin, "but you see, my ox is strong!"

"Bah!" said the merchant. "What else is new? Is it not the ox's nature to be strong?"

"Of course," stammered the poor Brahmin, "of course, but . . . but, not so strong as mine."

"Huh!" snorted the merchant, sipping his tea.

The Brahmin continued, "Why, this ox of mine is so strong he can pull 100 carts loaded to the top with boulders, gravel, and stone!"

"Impossible!" laughed the merchant. "Let me tell you something. No ox, no matter how strong, can pull such a load. After all," he added confidentially, "this world is one of weights and measures. An ox is, after all, just an ox. Like everything else, it has its necessary limits. No, my friend. This cannot be done."

"But it can!" insisted the Brahmin.

"It can't!" persisted the merchant.

"Let us wager," said the Brahmin.

"If you wish," said the merchant.

"One thousand pieces of silver?" suggested the Brahmin.

"Very good!" said the merchant. "One thousand pieces of silver it is! Now, when shall we test this great ox of yours?"

"Tomorrow?" asked the Brahmin.

"Yes, tomorrow, by all means," said the merchant. "Tomorrow, in the square. Let us meet before the sun is above the mango trees. You bring this great ox of yours and I'll see to it that the loaded carts are waiting. Until then, my friend, good day." And with that the merchant rose and walked smiling from the shop.

Soon the whole town was alight with the news. "One thousand pieces!" said some. "One hundred carts!" exclaimed others. "One ox!" laughed the rest.

Money changed hands and bets were placed. And then, at last, all waited in expectation for the morning.

That night the Brahmin tossed and turned anxiously. Would he win? Would he lose? Could Great Joy really pull so many loaded carts? The odds, after all, were entirely against it. "Ah," he thought with dismay, "what utter foolishness my life is resting on!"

But in the morning he awoke brightly enough with the rising sun and went out at once to Great Joy's stall.

There stood Great Joy, waiting quietly for him as usual, flicking his long tail in the warm air and contentedly chewing the golden straw. His great dark eyes looked out mildly at the Brahmin, with such good humor in them as if to say, "So, today's the day, eh? Well, don't worry, my friend, all shall be well." But today the Brahmin was preoccupied. He rested his arms on the rough edge of the ox's stall and stared at this great, contented ox. Motes of straw dust danced in the warm sunlit air. Yet it was cool in the stable. Everything there seemed so solid, so ordinary. The thick mud walls, the wooden buckets, the yokes, the worn ropes and brushes—how real, how sturdy they all were today. The Brahmin thought, "Perhaps this bet—perhaps my whole life, who knows, has been just a dream!"

He shook himself. "Dream or no, there's work to be done!" he announced. And picking up a stiff brush, he began to slap and brush the hard muscles of Great Joy's broad back with all his strength, so that the dust rose up in clouds from the glossy hide.

Then, combed, brushed, and curried, Great Joy and the Brahmin set off together across the fields and down the dirt roads to the town.

They arrived just as the sun was rising to the top of the tallest mango tree. The square was packed with a noisy crowd. And there were the carts, waiting. The Brahmin was shocked! He had never seen so many carts! "What a fool I have been," he suddenly thought, "to have taken the advice

of a mere beast. What have I done? I am lost!" And, with a sinking feeling in the pit of his stomach, he stepped forward.

The crowd parted to let the Brahmin and his Great Joy through. They walked along the row of carts. The merchant was waiting for them. He stood, smiling, alongside the very first cart.

"So are you ready?" he asked.

"Certainly. Of course we are ready!" replied the Brahmin.

The merchant motioned and two men stepped from the crowd. Stooping, they lifted the massive yoke on to Great Joy's shoulders. They knotted the new ropes tightly. In a last rush, final bets were placed (and indeed, a few, seeing Great Joy, now shouted out, "The ox! The ox! My money on the ox!"). Then, complete silence fell.

It was so quiet you could hear the birds singing in the nearby trees. It was so quiet you could hear the sweep of Great Joy's tail. It was so quiet you could hear the buzzing of the glittering flies.

Unconcerned, Great Joy gently eyed the staring crowd and mildly watched the white clouds drifting slowly by. He shook his huge head and exhaled loudly, as if to say, "What's all the fuss?"

Then the Brahmin, feeling all eyes focused on them, stepped closer to Great Joy's side and, raising a whip, struck Great Joy sharply on the shoulder, crying out, "On, you beast! On, you wretch! Do as I say! Pull those carts! Show your strength!"

But when Great Joy felt the bite of the whip and heard the Brahmin's harsh words, his eyes opened wide. "What's this!" he thought to himself. "Blows and curses? Well, not for this ox!" Planting his hooves massively in the earth, he stood rooted like a tree. Despite all the shouts and threats, all the pulls and prods, he would not budge. Not even an

inch. He would not even try to pull those carts. He stood unmoved, resolute, beneath all the blows. The crowd laughed
and jeered; they threw clods of earth and stones; they
shouted and screamed. But Great Joy would not budge.

"Ah, my friend, my friend," spluttered the wealthy
merchant, tears of laughter streaming down his cheeks,
"you were certainly right! That is some, ha! ha! ha!, ox indeed!"

When the proddings and threats had at last ceased,
and the crowd had drifted away, the merchant, still dabbing
his wet eyes, had been paid ("Better luck next time!" he
joked), only then did Great Joy, at last, let himself be un-
hitched and led silently away, home.

Once there, the Brahmin put his head in his arms and
sobbed and sobbed with shame and grief. Then once again,
Great Joy came to the window and spoke clearly to him, saying, "Why do you weep, my friend?"

Between his broken breaths the Brahmin, in great bitterness, cried out, "How can you ask such a thing, you un-
grateful beast? What you told me to do, I have done. But, for
all your promises, I have lost everything. And it's all because
of you! Not only that, the wealthy merchant and the whole
town have laughed at me as well. You alone are responsi-
ble!"

But Great Joy said sadly, "Did I let you down? Let me
ask you something. Did I ever break any of your fences? Or
smash a pot? Or crack a plow?"

"No," said the Brahmin, raising his head. "You never
did."

"Did I then, perhaps, ever step on or injure you or hurt
any of the children?"

"No," said the Brahmin once again. "Never!"

"Perhaps, then, I may have tracked mud into the
clean places of your home or before some sacred shrine?"

"No," repeated the Brahmin a third time. "You never

did anything like that either. You have always been a great joy to me."

"Then why," asked Great Joy the ox, "did you strike me and call me 'wretch' and 'beast'? Was this indeed the reward I deserved—I who wanted only to work hard for you?"

The Brahmin wiped his eyes and sat erect. In silence he looked at the ox and, knowing the truth of his words, grew ashamed.

"You are right," he said at last. "It was actually I who let you down. And I am sorry."

"Well," said the Ox, not unkindly, "since you now feel this way, let us try again. But this time you must bet 2,000 pieces."

"My friend!" cried the Brahmin, "I shall do my best. It shall be just as you say!"

"And I too shall do my best," said the Ox. "For if you don't let me down, I will certainly not let you down."

The next day the Brahmin ran to the town and entered the tea shop once again. There was the merchant calmly sipping his tea and eating his sweets.

"My I join you?" asked the Brahmin.

"By all means," said the merchant, merrily. "Have you not brought me great joy?"

"Let us bet again," said the Brahmin.

"What!" cried the merchant, astonished, "My friend, don't you know when you are beaten?"

"Come," said the Brahmin calmly, "one last wager, on the ox and the carts as before. But this time let us bet 2,000 pieces."

"Well, really," thought the merchant to himself, "fools like this don't grow on every tree." At last he shrugged, "Who am I to say no?"

"So, it's a wager?" asked the Brahmin.

"If you wish," said the merchant, smiling.

"Yes, I do wish," said the Brahmin, delighted. "Tomorrow in the square, at the same time as before. Tomorrow, my friend." And then he departed, wishing the merchant a good day.

The next morning the Brahmin once again curried Great Joy and brushed and cleaned him. Then, once again, he led his mighty ox to the center of the town.

Once more the crowd gathered, ready for some fun. But as Great Joy was led up to the carts, spiritedly tossing his great, horned head, sunlight suddenly sparkled like fire upon him and power pulsed from his shining back. His tail seemed to lash the skies like a dragon's tail and his wide, curved horns seemed to tear at the clouds. Each hair of his glossy, red-brown hide bristled and crackled and lifted electrically. The power of 1,000 breaths flowed from him and pulsed through the surging crowd, pouring from his heavy hooves into the dark earth and from his curling tail into the bright morning air. The crowd gasped. "What an ox!" they cried. "Perhaps he will be able to do it!"

Once again the heavy yoke was set upon him; once again the thick, new ropes were firmly tied. Then the Brahmin, stepping up to his ox's side, hung a wreath of flowers around Great Joy's massive neck, patted him on a giant shoulder and said quietly, "Now is the time, my mighty friend. This is the moment, my great-hearted ox; so pull, my brother, pull, my Great Joy, and let the whole world see your noble strength."

And with those kind, encouraging words, Great Joy happily planted his hooves firmly in the warm earth and stiffened his legs till they stood as strongly as ancient trees. Then he pulled and pulled and PULLED, straining and struggling with every muscle and every nerve until slowly, steadily, the wheels began to turn. Inch by inch, bit by bit, the carts rolled forward. "They move! They move!" cried the astonished crowd. "The carts begin to move!" Faster and faster and faster rolled the carts as Great Joy pulled and

pulled and pulled. The wealthy merchant's eyes opened wide. His jaw dropped in disbelief and the silver coins slipped from between his fingers into the dust. It wasn't possible! It couldn't be! But, "He's done it!" cried the crowd. "The ox has won!"

Still gathering speed, Great Joy pulled the carts right around the square and out through the gates of the town! Rolling, rolling, rolling, he circled the village and pulled all 100 loaded carts back through the gates and into the square once again.

And all the people followed, laughing wildly, slapping each other on the back and flinging their shirts high up into the air. For never, no never, had they seen or heard of such a wild and marvelous thing. The wealthy merchant, gathering his silver coins once again, ran, too. And so, of course, did the poor Brahmin. Truly, that day, the self-respecting ox, with his dignity and strength, gave them all great joy.

Now some say it must have been a pretty small town to have made such a fuss over an ox and some carts. But others (and, I think, wiser) say that it's always important when anyone, man or beast, shows us that there are no limits, when we find our own way, and when our hearts are really in it. What do you think?

The Monkey's Heart

Once
there was

a lazy and slow-witted crocodile who liked nothing better than to lie in the sun on the warm, muddy banks of his lazy, green river. He would stretch out at the water's edge and, shutting his eyes tight, open his mouth wide in a great toothy grin. Then the little birds would fly in and out of his jaws, pecking at the scraps of food stuck between his yellowed teeth. "Ah," he thought contentedly, digging his claws into the soft, gray mud, "this is the life!"

One day his wife crawled up to him and said, "Dear, have you noticed that large monkey swinging around on the island lately?"

"Uh-huh," grunted the crocodile, keeping his eyes shut and his mouth open wide.

"Well," she went on, "he looks quite large and juicy. I bet his heart is very tender. Oh," she said at last, "I wish I had that monkey's heart! Dear," she concluded "wouldn't you please go get that monkey's tender heart for me?"

"Uh-huh," sighed the crocodile, knowing that he'd have no peace until he'd gotten his wife what she wanted. Closing his jaws with a snap, he quietly opened his cold, yellow eyes and slowly crawled down the bank into the river. He moved his broad tail from side to side and slid through the cool, green water with hardly a ripple. But he was only halfway across when he realized he didn't know how to catch a monkey at all. Slowly he swung around and swam back to where his wife was now sunning herself. Her eyes were shut tight and her pink mouth was open wide.

"Dear," he said.

"Uh-huh?" she said.

"Well," he said, "how am I going to catch that monkey when he's way up in the trees and I'm down here in the water?"

"Well," she answered, "you're big and strong, aren't you?"

"Uh-huh!" he exclaimed.

"Well, then," she said, "just offer to carry him across on your back to where all the sweet coconuts are ripening. Be his friend. You can do that, can't you?" she said.

"Uh-huh!" he said. And then, once again, the crocodile turned around and slid back into the water. Slowly he swam off, moving his broad tail steadily from side to side.

At this time, the monkey was swinging around on his island, eating sweet fruits and enjoying himself in the warmth of the sun. "Ah," he reflected as he sat among the bright green leaves and fluttering orange butterflies, "but life is good!"

Now just at that moment, the crocodile reached the shores of the monkey's island. Crawling up on the sandy beach, he raised his knobbed and scaly head up toward the trees and called out in a very gentle-sounding voice indeed, "Oh brother monkey! Brother monkey!"

"Yes," answered the monkey, "what is it? Who is calling me?"

"It's me," said the crocodile, "your friend from across the river, the crocodile. I was just thinking, the day is so warm and bright and the sun is shining so gloriously, that I'd like to do something nice for a friend today. It's the perfect day for a swim, and my wife has told me that the coconuts are at last tender and juicy and ripe. I'd be glad to give you a ride over to where the sweetest ones are so you

can eat to your heart's content. In fact," added the crocodile with a toothy grin, "I'd be really glad to do it. Won't you come along?"

"I don't know," said the monkey, scratching his head and sitting down on his branch. "Let me think it over."

"It is a nice day," he thought to himself, "and ripe coconuts would be nice. Well," he asked, "will you promise to go slow?"

"Slow!" exclaimed the crocodile with an even toothier grin. "Why, certainly I'll go slow! Why," he added confidentially, "slow is my middle name. Come along. You'll see."

"Hmm," thought the monkey, "he seems kind enough and he's got such a nice smile. I'll go, but I'd better stay alert all the same."

"All right," said the monkey at last. "I'll go with you." Then he hopped out of the tree onto the crocodile's leathery back, and off they swam together across the river.

As they swam along, the little waves washed and rippled over the crocodile's green hide, splashing among the rough scales and wetting the monkey's hands and feet. "Ooh, it's cold!" he cried.

"Cold?" leered the crocodile with a cruel grin. "You call that cold? Why, that's not cold, that's not cold yet at all!" And with that he dived down through the green water to the gray, muddy bottom of the river. The terrified monkey held on tight—TIGHT—and when they broke the surface again in a burst of mud and foam, the poor monkey gasped out from between his chattering teeth, "Oh, friend crocodile, what are you doing? You nearly drowned me with your joke! Please, be more careful. Have you forgotten your promise? Remember, my home is in the trees!"

"What joke?" said the crocodile with another nasty grin. "I'm taking you back to my wife. She wants your tender heart. And what she wants, she gets!"

"Oh," said the monkey slowly, "I see, I see! Well, brother," he added after a moment, "it's a good thing you told me. You almost made a terrible mistake."

"I did?" asked the crocodile, concerned. The smile left his jaws. "Uh, tell me, friend monkey, how?"

"Why," said the monkey, "everyone knows that I don't take something as important as my tender heart along with me on these little, ordinary, everyday kind of trips. Oh, no. Not at all. Except for special occasions, I leave it hanging safely at the top of the tallest fruit tree of my island. Look back, brother, can't you see it hanging there on that tall tree right by the shore?"

Well, the crocodile thought that maybe he could see it, now that the monkey had pointed it out to him. Yes, he was sure. There it was! He did see it! What a mistake he had almost made!

"Listen, friend crocodile," said the monkey, "now that I know the whole story, why don't we just turn around. I'll go get my heart for you. It'll be no trouble at all. In fact, it'll just take a minute. I'll bet your wife would have been pretty upset," he added, as the crocodile turned slowly in the water and began to swim back to the island once again, "if you had brought me back without it."

"You're right," agreed the crocodile sadly, "she never would have understood. You know, for a monkey, you are a very good fellow."

"Thank you," said the monkey. "Glad I could help. If only you had told me sooner what you really wanted, everything would have been so much simpler. Well, no harm done, for here we are. Be back in a minute; enjoy the view!" And with that the monkey took a tremendous leap straight off the crocodile's back and bounded up into the branches of the tallest tree. Up, up, up he went, straight to the very top. And there, dancing on the highest branch, he now called out to the foolish crocodile far below, "Foolish, foolish

crocodile, tender hearts don't grow on trees! My true tender heart is not even that red fleshy fruit that hangs from the branching veins of my body. No! No! It is the heart of compassion which feels for all creatures—even for you, you silly crocodile. And, while it is not something which can be plucked at or taken away, it can still be yours, as one day even you shall see! So, farewell, my foolish friend. Never again will you catch me riding on your back. Not, that is, until you and your wife have both gained this great, true, tender heart for your own. Grin on, my toothy friend. Too bad, the joke's on you!"

And with that, the defeated crocodile swam off, embarrassed and confused.

The wise monkey sat in the warmth of the golden sunshine, drying his wet fur. The sweet fruits hung from the sturdy branches around him; the clear waves lapped against the sparkling grains of sand on the shore below. "Ah," he sighed, "how could that foolish crocodile have ever failed in finding my heart?"

The Wise Quail and the Foolish Quail

Once
there was

a wise quail. He lived in an ancient forest and was the leader of the flock. Through his guidance, all the birds were able to live in safety and contentment.

One day, unknown to the quails, a hunter came into their forest. Imitating the birds' own calls, he tricked them into approaching near him, and he stealthily began to trap the most unwary birds. After a while, the wise quail noticed that some of his flock were missing.

He called all the quails together and announced, "I think that a hunter is now in our forest. From this moment on, we must be extra-alert and extra-ready to help one another. Danger lurks on all sides. Know that our freedom, if not our very lives, will be threatened in the days ahead. Still," he added reassuringly, "if we all work together and cooperate, this hunter will not be able to hold us. We shall remain free. Let me tell you my plan."

And then the wise quail told them his thought, saying, "If you are scratching around for seeds or other food and you suddenly hear a whistling call 'twe whee! twe whee!' you might think it to be the call of a brother or sister. Then, if you go running off, and suddenly, darkness descends before your eyes and you find yourself trapped, unable to move, and the fear of death comes falling upon your heart— know that you have been tricked by the hunter's call and have been trapped in his cruel net! Still, if you do not give up, but follow my instructions, even then, you shall be free. Listen! When the net is upon you and all hope of flight seems gone, DO NOT GIVE UP! Look for the light shining between the dark webs of the heavy net. Stick your heads out there, through the spaces in the net where the light is still shining. Then, flap your wings, all together. If you flap hard, the net will rise off the ground. Fly with the net to a nearby bush. Let the net drape over the tough outer leaves and stems. Then all of you flutter out, down through the branches of the bush, and fly, each this way and that, to freedom. Will you do this?"

"We'll do it!" cried all the quails. "We'll work together and keep our lives and freedom!"

"Good!" said the wise quail. "I am very happy to think that my flock will be safe."

As it happened, the very next day, some of the quail were out pecking around for their food when they heard a loud, whistling call—"twe whee! twe whee! twe whee!"—and, thinking that one of their brother or sister quail was calling them, they went running off to see what had happened. Suddenly, darkness descended before their eyes and their wings were pinned by the cords of the hunter's net. But then they remembered the words of the wise quail. Thrusting their heads through the spaces of the net, they all flapped their wings together, harder and harder, and slowly, slowly, the net rose off the ground, just as the wise quail had said it would. Beating, beating, beating the air, the quails flew with the net to a bush, settled on the bush, let the net drape over it, and then, scurrying out, each flew away, this way and that, to freedom. They were safe! The plan had worked! How happy they were to have escaped from the jaws of death!

But the hunter was not happy. Try as he would, he could not understand how the quails had managed to escape. And his wife wasn't happy either. Oh no, that hunter

would not have an easy time of it again until he brought home more quail. So he watched and watched and thought and thought and at last came to the conclusion, after many days of finding his empty nets draped over the nearby bushes, that the quails were cooperating. "They are working together!" he thought to himself, amazed. "That's why I've not been able to catch them! Well, that won't last forever. They are only birds, and featherbrains at that. Sooner or later they will start to argue. And when they do, when they do," he muttered, "I'll have them. Yes, all I have to do is be patient. They will do the rest."

Now the wise quail had had the same thought. In time, the quails would grow lazy and forget that their lives and freedom depended on their working together. After reflecting on the danger, he decided that he and his flock should go to a more isolated part of the forest. There, in greater seclusion, and in less danger, they could really learn how to cooperate. They could practice working together. Then they would be truly free.

Sure enough, that very day something happened that confirmed the wise quail's thought. And this is what it was:

A quail was pecking among the thinly scattered grass blades when, from above, another quail began to flap his wings slowly, descending from the sky. As this second quail came down, he accidentally brushed the face of the other quail with the flaring, finger-like feathers of his wing tip. At once the first quail yelled out, "Hey! Watch it, stupid!"

"Who are you," said the quail who had landed, flustered because he had been so clumsy, "to call me stupid? Why, you were too dumb to get out of my way!"

"What! Me too dumb!" shouted the first quail, quite angry now. "Why, you don't even know how to land without hitting someone in the face! If that's not dumb, I don't know what is!"

"Well, what about you?" shouted back the other bird.

"How smart is it to just stand there, pecking blindly away when someone else is trying to land? Ever hear of moving, birdbrain?"

"Birdbrain! Birdbrain is it?" screamed the first quail in a rage. "Why, you're the birdbrain. Who ever taught you to fly? Bats?"

"Bats is it? Bats!" screamed the second bird, also totally enraged. "I'll give you a bat, you feathered ninny!" And with a loud chirping whistle, he threw himself at the other quail, who fluttered quickly away. They chased each other among the trees and through the glade, hurling insults and threats. And so it went. Back and forth. An argument had begun and, as is the way of arguments, no end was in sight.

Now the wise quail, some distance away, heard the argument and knew at once that danger was upon them. He called all the quail together and told them, "This section of the forest is no longer safe for us. We must go further into the forest, and there, in greater safety, learn how to get along with one another. We've got to work at it and practice it together. Then, when disagreements do arise, we'll be ready; we'll be able to resolve them before bitter words are spoken or blows are struck. Only then will we be safe from the hunter's nets. Remember, our freedom depends on our working together. Well, my quails, will you come with me?"

And many of the birds said, "Yes, Wise Quail, we will come with you!"

But some of the quails said, "Hey, what's the big deal? We know how to escape from the hunter! Why, you taught us yourself! Sure," they said, "we just put our heads through the net, flap our wings, land on a bush, flutter out, and fly away. It's easy! Any dumb cluck would know how to do that. And, speaking of dumb, it's dumb to move. We like it here. We're going to stay!"

So the wise quail and those who were willing to go

with him left that part of the forest. But the others stayed.

A few days later, the quails who had decided to stay were pecking around, scratching up their dinner, when they heard an urgent, whistling call, "twe whee! twe whee! twe whee!" They ran to it. Suddenly, darkness descended before their eyes and fear overcame them. They were trapped in the hunter's net! Then they remembered the wise quail's teaching. They stuck their heads through the spaces in the netting and one of them said, "Okay, now when I count to three we all flap. Ready? One, two, thr . . . "

"Hey!" shouted another bird. "Who made you boss? Who said you could give the orders around here?"

"What do you mean?!" said the first bird. "I'm the hardest worker, so, of course, I should give the orders. Why, when I flap my wings I flap so hard that the dust flies up to the clouds. That's how hard I work and that's why I should be the one to give the orders. So there!"

"Ha!" exclaimed another bird. "That's nothing! Why, when I flap my wings, I flap so hard that the sweat just rolls down my beak and forms streams in the dusty earth! That's how hard I work. So if anyone should be giving the orders around here, it's me!"

"No, me!" shouted a third bird.

"No, me!" shouted yet a fourth.

"Listen to me!" shouted the first bird once again above the rising din. "Flap! Flap! Flap! I tell you! Everybody flap your wings! Everybody flap together! When I say 'three'!"

But no one flapped. They all just argued, back and forth. And, as they argued, the hunter just rolled up his net and carried them all off to his home. And their fate, I'm sad to say, was not a happy one.

But the other quails, the ones who had gone off deeper into the safety of the great forest worked hard and learned to cooperate. Whenever arguments arose, they tried to resolve them. Showing respect for one another, they undercut anger and mistrust before it could arise. And so, under the wise quail's guidance they grew in wisdom and strength. And because they always worked together, no one ever took their freedom from them. And if no one ever took their freedom from them, why, it stands to reason, they're still free today.

Prince
Five-Weapons

Once,
many long ages ago,

the Bodhisattva was born as the son of a noble king. When he was sixteen years of age, his father said to him, "It's time you went to the city of Takkasila. Find a teacher there, master the five weapons, and return. You shall help me rule the kingdom. Now, when can you start on your journey?"

"Why, with the morning light, Father," said the prince.

And so, the next day, just as the sun rose and the birds began to sing, the prince set off for Takkasila, that ancient city famed for its warriors, wise men, and weapons-masters.

He walked for many days. He traveled through forests, over mountains, and across many swift rivers and streams. At last, the famous city lay before him. He wandered through the winding streets and along the broad avenues and markets, observing the people carefully and calling on noted warriors and teachers. At last he found one who impressed him. Though old and white-bearded, the weapon-master was as straight and strong and limber as a young tree.

The prince stayed in Takkasila and worked hard to master the arduous training. Each day he arose before dawn and went at once into the practice yard. And there he stayed until evening. Only when the first stars were twinkling in the deepening blue of the sky above would he return to his room, and drop, exhausted, into his narrow bed again. And, in between, it was cut and slash and hammer and parry until his bones grew hard as iron, and his movements, as practiced and smooth as thrice-polished silver.

One day the old weapons-master said to him, "Young Prince, you have indeed gained skills in all five weapons. What's more, you are accomplished and disciplined. The time has come for you to return to your own kingdom. Now you are ready to aid your faither and learn a ruler's ways." And he gave the prince the name Prince Five-Weapons.

The prince thanked his teacher for his guidance and wisdom. Then, shouldering the five weapons, he set off for his home.

After several days' march he came upon a barricade blocking the way, just where the path narrowed and entered a dark forest. Armed men stood by the barricade. "Stop!" they called out. "Do not enter the forest by this road," they warned. "Go some other way. A horrible monster named Sticky-Hair lives along this road. He terrifies travelers and gobbles them up! Go back, young prince! Find some other way through! This way may cost you your life!"

But the prince just laughed and pushed boldly forward. "What's this you say?" he asked. "A monster dwells here? Why should a monster stop one who is skilled and free? After all," he said, "I've trained in the five-weapons. I'm not going to run away from danger. I've spent these last years in hard work, learning to be of some good in this world. No," he said, "I'll take this road. When I'm through here, the way will be open again for everyone to travel on."

So, despite their warnings, he slipped around the barricade of hewn logs and strode down the very center of the forest path.

As the prince walked on, the trees grew taller and thicker, and the surrounding bushes, more wildly tangled with every step. So, the further he walked, the darker his path became.

56

But let me ask you. Was the prince frightened? Was he fearful or downcast? No! Of course not! He wasn't frightened at all. He just walked steadily on.

Soon the trees were so high that they arched over the road, almost blocking out the blue sky. Many unknown rustlings, creakings, and scurryings sounded from the bushes all around him. An owl hooted, "Whoo! Whoo!" from within the tangled gloom and a black crow flapped across the path before him.

Suddenly a terrible, huge, glaring head appeared above the tops of the tallest trees! It was Sticky-Hair, the monster! He was immense, wild and horrible to see! His eyes, as large as the windows of a house, glowed like coals! Each nostril, dark as the entrance to a cave, shot flames! His teeth were like jagged boulders and his hands large as carts. Each sharp fingernail curved like a scimitar.

"Well," announced the prince, "so it is you I have come to meet. Be warned," he said, fitting an arrow to his bow, "that I am Prince Five-Weapons and I am here to make this road safe. So, either change your ways," he added, drawing the bowstring back to his cheek, "or be prepared to meet your doom."

But the monster, Sticky-Hair, only laughed horribly in a booming voice and took another giant step closer to the prince. "Ha! Ha! Ha!" he chortled as closer and closer and CLOSER he came.

Then the prince, aiming straight at the monster's heart, released his arrow. Straight as a falcon it flew, straight toward the monster's cruel heart. TTHuuup! It struck! But the arrow only hung there. It was stuck to the monster's sticky hair. It hadn't hurt him at all!

"Oh, so that's how it is," said the prince, fitting another arrow to the string. Then, drawing his powerful bow back smoothly once again, Whooosh! he let another arrow fly, straight at the monster's heart. But that arrow only stuck there, too! Then the prince shot another arrow and another and another; TTHuuup! TTHuuup! TTHuuup! He shot fifty sharp arrows in all, straight and true at the monster's heart. But they, too, just stuck to the monster's sticky, sticky hair. Not a single one had hurt the monster at all!

How the monster laughed and roared. He showed his pointed, yellow teeth. He shook himself like a wet dog until the arrows rattled together and flew off in every direction. Then, once again, he stepped forward, toward the prince.

But, let me ask you, was the prince afraid? No! Of course not! The prince was not afraid at all!

Standing his ground, he lifted up his heavy spear and hurled it with all his might, straight at the monster's heart. But the spear, too, just hung there, stuck to the monster's sticky hair. It didn't hurt the monster at all. He just kept coming closer and closer and closer. Then the prince drew his sword. The blade flashed as he swung it fearlessly with all his strength. But what was this? The sword, too, just stuck to the monster's sticky hair.

But was the prince daunted? Was he frightened or cast down? No! No! He was not! Bold as ever, he lifted his heavy ironwood club, all gnarled and knotted like an immense fist, and swinging it once, twice, three times, smashed it with all his strength into the monster's knee! But the club, too, just stuck to the sticky, sticky hair. It didn't hurt the monster at all.

"Ha!" said the prince. "When I came into this forest, I didn't just trust in my weapons. No! Not at all! I trusted in myself. And because I trust in myself, I'm not going to give up now. Why, if I have to, I'll smash that monster to dust with my own two fists!"

And, drawing back with his right fist, the brave prince struck a furious blow. But his fist, too, just stuck to the monster's coat of sticky, sticky hair.

Then the prince drew back with his left fist and let

loose another tremendous blow. If the monster had only been a huge tree, even a great forest oak, the prince's punch would have crashed it, splintering, to the ground. Or if that monster had been a massive granite boulder, that punch would have smashed it into a thousand glittering pieces. But the monster was, of course, himself. He was protected by his sticky hair. So the prince's mighty blow did not hurt him at all. And now the prince's left fist, too, was stuck to the monster's coat of sticky hair.

It was a grim moment. Both the prince's hands were stuck, and the monster, with a nasty grin that showed all his crooked, yellow teeth, was reaching out to grab the prince and gobble him up.

But, let me ask you, was the prince afraid? Did he tremble or cry out? No! He did not! For he was not afraid. He was not afraid at all!

Drawing back with his right leg, he lashed out a mighty, bone-shattering kick. But, of course, it didn't hurt the monster at all. And now the prince's foot was stuck to the monster's sticky hair.

Drawing back with his left leg, Whack! he kicked out fiercely, like a tiger leaping at its prey. But his left foot too just stuck to the sticky hair.

"Well," said the prince, "the time has finally come for me to use my head." So, arching his neck, he drew back his head and launched a terrible, crashing blow. But, I'm sad to say, his head, too, just stuck to the monster's thick coat of sticky hair.

Now the prince was completely stuck. Like a fly caught by flypaper, he was trapped. His head, hands, and feet were stuck. He hung from the monster's sticky hair, unable to move at all.

But still the prince wasn't afraid. He wasn't afraid at all! And the monster could sense this. He could feel that the prince was confident, with no fear in him.

Because of this, the monster grew frightened. He became hesitant and unsure. "Never," he thought to himself, "never have I met such a man, such a lion, such a hero! Why," he thought "everyone else I've met turned and ran as soon as they saw me. Then I grabbed them and gobbled them up! But this warrior-prince just came straight on. He didn't turn and he didn't run. And now that I've caught him and he's completely stuck, he's still unafraid. What's he up to?" thought the monster nervously to himself. "I don't like this; something's suspicious here. Aha!" exclaimed the monster with a start. "He must have some magic weapon and if I tried to devour him it would destroy me. I'd better ask him before it's too late!"

"Ahem, Prince?" asked the monster.

"Yes!" said the prince.

"Oh, well," said the monster, "I was just wondering if, ahem, well, if you have some secret, er, weapon about you that is making you so unafraid."

"Yes!" said the prince, "I do!"

"I thought so," lamented the monster. "Ah," he continued, "what is it?"

"I have a sword of truth in my belly," said the prince. "If you try to eat me, it will cut you to pieces and I will jump out unharmed and free!"

"Oh," said the monster, "I believe you! Don't do anything rash! I'm letting you go!" And he lifted the prince from the sticky hair and set him on the ground. The prince stood free, once more, like the shining moon when it is released from the darkness of the clouds.

"But," said the prince when he had stepped from the monster's grasp, "I do not release you. Listen. You have become a miserable monster because you treated others so cruelly in your past lives. If you were kinder, your life would be happier."

"I have been pretty miserable," said the monster.

"Well," said the prince, "if you started being kind, and kept at it life after life, you would become happier and wiser. In time, you wouldn't be a monster any longer. You would become a free and noble person, a real human being. A whole new world would open to you."

"I believe you!" exclaimed the monster, Sticky-Hair.

"Good!" said the prince. "I'm happy to hear it."

"And from now on," continued the monster, "I will protect wayfarers on the road! I won't injure anyone ever again. I'll be the guardian of this dark forest path, and help travelers whenever I can."

"Excellent!" said the prince. "You're on the right track. Farewell, for now. But, remember, I'll be back from time to time to see how things are going."

Then, gathering up his arrows and his sword, and shouldering his spear, club, and bow, Prince Five-Weapons marched on, down the forest road.

When he reached the other side of the forest he called out to the astonished men guarding that entrance, "The way is clear! The path is open! The monster Sticky-Hair is no more! A guardian now dwells along this forest path! Tell travelers they can expect help from him in times of danger." And, striding on, he came at last to his father's kingdom.

Years later, when his father, the old king, died, Prince Five-Weapons became king in his place. He was a wise and brave ruler. His people liked to call him King Five-Weapons, "The Opener of the Ways." He lived to a ripe age. Then, in time, he too passed on to a new birth, as all living things do, in accordance with his thoughts and deeds.

As for the monster. Why, he, of course, followed Prince Five-Weapons' instructions faithfully. Acting kindly, he grew happier—just as the prince had said he would. Lifetime after lifetime he guarded the ways until, just recently, he was born as the son of a good man and woman right here in our own city!

The Goose
with the
Golden Feathers

Once
there was

a poor man. He lived with his wife and two children—a boy and a girl—in a small thatched cottage at the forest's edge.

For some reason, this man fell ill. He grew weaker and weaker. As he lay dying, a single thought filled his mind. "If I must now die I wish at least somehow to be of help to my family."

This was his last conscious wish and, soon afterwards, he died.

His wife and children were grief-stricken and filled with worry. How would they live without their kind husband and father?

That night, the children had a dream. They saw their father once again. "Dear children," he told them, "do not grieve. I will be back with you soon. I cannot say if I shall be a man or bird or beast when I return. But this I will say. You'll know me by a great, shining light."

The children awoke, their eyes bright, and ran to tell their mother. But she only laughed bitterly when they told her the dream. "No," she said, "no, my little ones. What is gone stays gone—forever. Forget your dream. Our lot will be hard enough without such dreams."

So the children didn't speak of the dream to their mother again. But between themselves, they spoke of it.

One evening, several months later, as the sun dropped below the trees, a strange light shone through the branches. The leaves gleamed and seemed to turn to gold. Something was coming along the forest path.

The children looked at one another and then ran out to meet whatever might be coming.

A large white goose with golden eyes and yellow legs waddled into the clearing. Stretching out its neck, it honked loudly in a human voice, "Children, it is I!"

"Father! Father!" they cried. "It is you! We saw the light! Just as you said in the dream!"

"Yes!" said the goose, "I have come to help you, as I promised. But oh, it is good to see you!" He wrapped his wings around the two children who knelt by him. "How big you have grown! Hush now," he said at last, "and listen. You must promise me that you won't tell anyone who I am."

"We promise."

"Good. Now, listen carefully again. Every day, just as the sun rises above these trees, you must pluck one of my feathers and hold it up to the sunlight. The feather will turn to pure, gleaming gold. In this way, you and your mother will never lack for anything. But remember, you must tell no one, not even your mother, who I am. And you must be careful to pluck only one feather each day."

"We'll remember," said the children.

"But, Father," asked the girl, "won't it hurt you when we pluck your feathers?"

"Yes," said the boy, "we couldn't do it if it hurt you."

"Don't worry, children," honked the goose. "Every feather you pluck will quickly grow back and as long as you pluck only one at a time, no harm at all shall come to me. It is my gift to you and your mother. Now, quickly," said the goose, "before the sun sinks below the trees, pluck a feather!"

So they reached out together and plucked a short, downy feather from the goose's breast. They held it up to the sun's last rays and at once it turned to pure, gleaming gold!

66

They ran to their mother. "Look, Mother! Look!" they cried. "We have a feather of pure gold and fath . . . er, . . . the goose said that we shall be able to have all we want, too!" And, joining hands, the two children began to dance around and around the astonished woman.

"What are you saying?" she cried. "Where did you get such a bright feather? Why!" she cried, "It's gold! Pure gold!"

"Yes!" they cried. "Of course, it's gold! Just as the goose said!"

"What goose?" asked their mother, placing the golden feather carefully on the table.

"Why, the goose in our yard," said the children. "Come, mother," they said, taking her hands. "Come, come see."

There stood the goose watching them quietly from the very center of the yard. "Why, it's a handsome goose," said the mother, "but its feathers aren't gold."

"No," said the boy, "the feathers only turn to gold when you pluck them."

"And," said the girl, "you must pluck only one feather each day."

Naturally, their mother found this hard to believe. But, as she had no other explanation for the golden feather, she agreed to wait and see. She closed the gate, so the goose wouldn't wander away, then returned to the little thatched house.

The children stayed out in the yard and played with the goose until it grew dark, and the stars twinkled out in the clear night sky. They petted the goose and talked to it. But, though the goose seemed delighted with their company, though it wrapped them in its wings and lay its head and neck against them, and touched their hands and feet and cheeks lightly with its orange beak, it only honked and gabbled. Not once did it speak to them again in human words.

Still, as it was clear that the goose loved them, they went to bed content.

The next morning, when the sun rose bright as gold above the tops of the tallest trees, the little family gathered in the yard. The children held the goose tenderly. Then, as the sun's rays fell upon them, their mother bent down and pulled a long feather from the bird's wing. She held it up to the sunlight.

At once the feather turned to solid gold.

The mother gasped and almost dropped the feather. "Ah," she cried, "so, it's true!"

"Yes! Yes, mother!" cried the two children. "Of course, it's true! We told you! We told you!"

"Well," she said recovering herself, "we must feed this goose well. We shall not starve after all! This goose is our benefactor. We must take good care of it!"

And that's what they did.

Every day, just as the sun rose above the trees, the little family gathered in the bare, dirt yard and plucked one of the goose's feathers. And, as the sun's rays touched the feather, it turned to gold. Soon the mother began to buy good food and new clothes for them all. Then she bought shining copper pots and polished ladles of dark, smooth wood. She bought little mirrors and she hung tinkling bells on the roof poles. She bought carved wooden animals for the children. After that, she plastered the walls of the cottage and fixed the door. She put a strong fence around the yard. She got chickens and built a henhouse and soon they were eating fresh eggs. Next she bought a buffalo to help them plow the fields and to give them its rich, sweet milk. She even bought a little golden dish from which the goose could eat.

They were content. And the goose seemed content, too. Every morning, after they pulled out a feather, it would flap its wings, stretch out its neck, and honk as if for joy. Then, after it had eaten, and preened itself, the goose would

even follow the children out into the fields and return with them at twilight.

One night, the mother awoke in the darkness. As she lay there she could hear her children breathing peacefully in their sleep beside her. She reflected on their extraordinary luck. Who would have imagined that a goose with feathers that turned to gold would suddenly appear and save them from hardship! It was a miracle! And now, by storing the feathers and trading them wisely, they would be able to have all they might ever need—or want. Outside, in the darkness, the buffalo snorted in its stall and night birds called. The woman smiled and dozed off again to sleep.

But, as life became less burdensome, the mother found it harder to be content. "Why," she thought, "we've got a living gold mine waddling around out there, honking, in our yard! One feather at a time keeps us secure, it is true. But, if we plucked the whole bird, all at once, we would be rich. We could buy whatever we wanted and go wherever we wished. And indeed, we should move soon. The neighbors have already begun to wonder where we are getting our money. Once they learn of the goose, someone will try to steal him. "How can I be content with this tiny trickle of gold, when I could wash away all our cares forever by plucking the whole bird!"

The children begged her to be content with what they already had. "Our life is secure," they said. "We have all we need. We can make our own way now, thanks to the golden goose, Mother. Besides, the goose told us we must pluck only one feather at a time. It would hurt him if we plucked them all. Please," they said, "please promise us that you won't pluck the goose." So, in the end, the mother agreed.

But again the desire for all the gold rose within her. "It's only a goose, after all," she reasoned. "Why should I be concerned? And though children have tender hearts, they soon forget. I'll be using the gold for their welfare anyway," she thought. "Surely that can't bring us any harm. As to plucking only one feather at a time," she thought on, "I've never heard the goose say that—or anything else for that matter!"

So, once again, she decided to pluck the whole goose. But again the children begged, pleaded, and cried. And again, she held off, discomfited and confused.

"It's a goose," she told herself, "just a goose. What do children know of life? How can I weigh a single goose against my family's welfare? It's ridiculous! Absurd!" So, at last, she made up her mind. And this time, she was determined. "I shall pluck it!" she said. "As a mother, I can protect my children best with gold."

That morning, just as the sun rose like red gold, the mother crept quietly out into the yard and caught the goose. While the children slept, she quickly pulled fistfuls of feathers from the uncomplaining bird who shivered uncontrollably, watching her all the while with sad, golden eyes. Feathers flew like whirling snow but still the woman plucked and plucked, stuffing the white feathers into a sack that she had at hand.

Pushing her hair back from her sweaty brow, she at last released the bare bird, which ran off and hid under the leafy bushes in the farthest corner of the yard. It seemed to her that as the bird ran off tears had trickled from its eyes, and that now, from beneath the leaves, came the sounds of soft sobbing.

With a shiver, the woman set her jaw and lifted the sack of feathers up to the golden light, just as the sun rose once again above the tallest trees.

The pure, golden light shone upon the sack. But the sack stayed as light as down. She lowered the sack and peered within. The feathers were all still soft and white. Not one had turned to gold.

The poor woman cried aloud. The children heard her

cry and ran out to the yard. Fistfuls of feathers blew from the open sack and across the yard like snow from the mountains.

"Oh, Mother!" they cried. "Oh, Mother, what have you done? The goose, the poor, poor goose! Oh, Father! Father! We promised we wouldn't tell, but, yes, it is our own father you have plucked so bare. Remember our dream? Well, he is the goose."

The mother sobbed and sobbed. "Well," she finally said, sniffling, "I don't know anything about that. Your poor father is gone forever, but feathers grow again." Blowing her nose loudly, she concluded, "We'll take good care of the goose and wait. Next time, I promise you, I shall pluck only one feather at a time."

But when the goose's feathers grew in again they were speckled and gray. And not one ever turned to gold.

The little family lived on. They worked hard and got by. Later, when the children had grown and set off into the world on their own, the goose spread its wings and flew away. And it was never seen again.

The woman grew old and lean and learned to be content with little. Eventually, she became known throughout the neighborhood for the simplicity of her life and for her hard work. "Don't be greedy!" she would say to everyone she met. "Everything comes in its own time."

Somehow, those who heard her took it to heart. Though her words were simple, everyone could tell that here, at last, was someone who really knew what she was talking about.

The Brave Little Parrot and the Eagle's Tears

Once,
long ages ago,

the Buddha was born as a friendly little parrot. He lived happily in the forest and delighted in flying among the tangled branches of the huge, forest trees. Wherever he went, he greeted other creatures with joy. He was a happy bird, glad to be alive and glad to have been given the gift of flight.

One day the skies over his forest home darkened and, without warning, a terrible storm thundered down, flashing and roaring among the ancient trees. The wind howled, lightning crackled, and one old tree burst into flames. Soon the whole forest began to blaze as sparks blew everywhere. Terrified animals ran wildly in every direction, seeking safety from the burning flames and choking, acrid smoke.

When the little parrot smelled the smoke, he flung himself out bravely into the fury of the storm, crying out loudly as he flew, "Fire! Fire! Run to the river!" But though the animals heard his voice and many did make it to the safety of the river, what could the others do, trapped as they were by the flames and smoke? So, rather than flying off to safety himself, he continued circling over the raging fire, seeking some means of helping those who were trapped below.

A desperate idea came to him. Darting down to the river that flowed at the forest's edge, he dipped his body and wings into the dark water and then flew back to the fire, which was now raging like an inferno. Unmindful of the leaping flames, he dropped down low and rapidly shook his wings, releasing the few precious drops of water which still clung to his feathers. They tumbled down like little jewels into the heart of the blaze. Again he flew to the river and dipped in body and wings and again he flew back over the flames. Again and again he flew between the river and the forest, many, many times. His feathers grew greasy and ragged and black and his eyes burned red as coals. His lungs ached and his mind danced dizzily with the spinning sparks, but still the brave little parrot flew on. "What, after all, can a bird do in times like these," he said to himself, "but fly? So fly I shall. And I won't stop if there's even a chance I can save a single life."

Now some of the godly beings of the higher realms, relaxing in their palaces of ivory and gold, saw the little parrot below them as he flew among the leaping flames. Between mouthfuls of sweet foods, they pointed him out. And some of them began to laugh. "What a foolish little bird!" they said. "Trying to put out a raging fire with just a few sprinkles of water from his wings. Who ever heard of such a thing? Why, it's absurd!"

But one of the gods found himself strangely moved by what he saw. Taking the form of a golden eagle, he let himself be drawn down into the parrot's fiery path.

The little parrot was just nearing the flames again when suddenly a huge eagle with eyes like molten gold appeared at his side. "Go back, little bird! Your task is hopeless!" pronounced the eagle in a solemn and majestic voice. "What can a few drops of water do against a blaze like this? Turn around and save yourself before it is too late!"

But the little parrot would not listen. He only continued to fly doggedly on through the flames. He could hear the great eagle flying above him now as the heat grew

fiercer, still calling out, "Stop! Stop! Foolish little parrot! Save yourself! Save yourself!"

But the little parrot only continued on. "Why, I don't need a great, shining eagle to give me advice like that!" he thought to himself. "My own mother, the dear bird, could have told me such things long ago. Advice," he coughed, "I don't need advice. I just need someone to pitch in and help!"

And the great eagle, seeing the little parrot flying so steadily on through the searing flames, thought with shame of his own privileged kind. He could see the carefree gods looking down from above as if life was just a game for others to live. He could hear their laughter still echoing, while many creatures cried out in fear and pain from the flames just below. All at once, he no longer wanted to be a god or an eagle or anything else. He simply wanted to be like that brave little parrot, and to help.

"I will help!" he said. And, flushed with these new feelings, he began to weep. Streams and streams of sparkling tears poured from his eyes and washed down in waves like cooling rain upon the fire, upon the forest, upon the animals, and upon the little parrot himself.

Deluged with the god's shimmering tears, the flames died down and the smoke began to clear. The little parrot himself, washed and bright, rocketed about the sky like a little feathered sun. He laughed aloud, "Now that's more like it!" Tears dripped quietly from all the burned branches and scorched buds, which began to send forth green shoots and stems and leaves.

Teardrops sparkled on the parrot's wings, too, and dropped down like petals upon the burned and blackened ground. Green grass began to push up from among the still glowing cinders.

Then all the animals looked at one another in amazement. All were whole and well. Up in the clear blue sky they could see their friend, the little parrot, looping and soaring and flying happily on and on. "Hurray!" they suddenly cried, "Hurray for the brave little parrot and for this sudden, miraculous rain!"

The Merchant's Walk

Once,
in days long gone by,

the Bodhisattva dwelt as a merchant in the royal city of Benares.

One morning, one of the solitary Buddhas of the mountains entered the city. Silently walking from house to house, he collected small offerings of food for his meal.

He arrived at the gate of the merchant's house and stood quietly there in great dignity and perfect calm.

The merchant looked up from his work within the courtyard. Seeing the humble beggar at his gate, he thought to himself, "Now there is someone at peace with himself and with all the world. He must be one of the solitary Buddhas of the mountains!" And gathering some of the best food in his house, he hurried to the wooden gate where the great sage was quietly waiting.

Suddenly Mara, the fiendish tempter who opposes all goodness, appeared. "If this merchant makes his offering, his faith will increase a thousandfold. Someday he too will enter the mountains and find his way beyond my power. I must stop him."

Then Mara made one of the great fiery hells open up before the merchant's feet. Flames leaped everywhere. Because of them the merchant could no longer see the Buddha standing just before him at the gate. Instead of the calling of birds and the noises of the street, the merchant could hear only screams.

Sweat poured down the merchant's body and his heart beat wildly with dread. Then he thought, "This is surely Mara's doing. He seeks to overcome me. Today we shall see who is stronger. For, hell or no hell, I will still make this offering." Taking a step forward, he fell into the flames.

Molten iron walls rose around him. Searing flames beat against him and hard, brassy voices laughed horribly, booming, "This is the end! This is the end of all things!" Bloody figures writhed on the ground and horrible, blood-curdling screams filled his ears.

The merchant, his hair standing on end, walked on. He walked on and on. Time stopped. He walked forever.

But suddenly, the hell vanished. Once again the sun shone brightly in a clear, blue sky. Birds sang sweetly in the green, swaying trees, and along the busy streets men and women hurried as before. It was over. The merchant had come safely through. Before him at the gate the Buddha still stood in an old, patched robe, holding out his worn wooden bowl to receive the merchant's offering. In fact, hardly an instant had passed.

Flushed and triumphant, but still trembling, the merchant made his offering and bowed. The solitary Buddha smiled and inclined his own head toward the courageous merchant. "Well done," he said. "Well done, indeed. Know, worthy merchant, that this life is like a dream. Gains and losses drift by like clouds. But to those who walk on, despite obstacles and fears, success comes at last. Walk on, good merchant, walk on! In this dream of a life we shall certainly meet again."

Then the solitary Buddha walked out of the royal city and returned to the silence of his high mountains.

And the merchant continued to work hard. Sharing his wealth with others, he walked on rightly through many years of life. And Mara never did stop him.

So we too should all walk on with faith. Dangers may appear and awful precipices yawn suddenly before us. Still, when we least expect it, a clear light will shine and the wild birds again will sing sweetly all around.

The Doe,
the Hunter, and
the Great Stag

Once

a great stag

with antlers like shining gold lived in the heart of a green forest. He was the leader of a herd of eighty deer. His doe was beautiful, too. She was slender and graceful. Her dark eyes shone like forest pools. The great stag and his wife, the doe, lived together in mutual respect and love.

One day a hunter came into the forest and set a wire snare along one of the forest trails. The great stag, leading the herd, stepped into the snare, which tightened around his leg, just above the hoof. He tried to tug free but the wire noose only cut deeper. He tugged again and the noose tightened even more cruelly into the flesh. He tugged a third time and now the tightening noose cut into the tendon and bone! With a cry, the great stag tumbled down into the dust, his leg caught and bleeding in the terrible trap.

His herd, hearing his cry of alarm, turned at once and fled. But the doe, his wife, thought, "My husband is in danger!" And she leapt forward. There lay the great stag, his sides heaving, struggling to rise, one bloody leg held tightly by a shiny metal noose.

"Get up, my Lord!" cried the doc. "Use your strength and snap the snare! We shall flee together before the hunter returns!"

But the great stag said, "The snare is too strong. I've

tried to break it. It's no use. I'm caught. Go now! Run before the hunter comes. There's nothing more you can do." Then he lay back, panting, in the dust of the trail.

"No!" said the doe. "I won't leave you. Either we both go free or neither of us will." She licked the stag's face and cleaned the matted fur of his bloodstained leg. Two tears rolled from her eyes.

Soon the hunter could be heard approaching, crashing loudly through the bushes nearby. The clanging of his spear blade against the loose stones of the path sounded, to the terrified doe, like the bone-piercing winds that end an eon. The cold smell of death and dried blood assailed her nostrils as the hunter came closer and closer.

"Run! Run!" cried the great stag to the doe. "Run now and be free. I cannot bear that you, my beloved doe, should die!"

But the gentle doe only shook her delicate head from side to side. Her eyes were wide with fright. She shivered and trembled. But still she said, "No. I will not leave."

The hunter's steps came closer and closer. The leafy branches by the side of the trail swayed violently; they bent, and, snapping, broke. Suddenly, the hunter, wearing an old, scarred deerskin jacket and gripping a short, stabbing spear in his hands, tore through the bushes before them.

"Why, what's this?" he exclaimed. "Two deer and one snare? I've never seen such a thing before!"

But the doe rose bravely and walked toward the man. "As you can see," she said, "I have not been caught by your snare, O man-who-smells-of-blood. I stay of my own free will. My husband, the leader of our herd, is trapped. I won't desert him. We have shared life. Now, if need be, we shall share what is called death. Yet, if pity resides within even your hard, human heart, take me alone. Spare my husband. All the other deer depend on him. To take him would mean

their deaths as well. Let him go free. I offer my own life in exchange."

The hunter was amazed and looked in wonder from the doe to the helpless, bloodstained stag and back again. His face softened and he stabbed his spear, point down, into the earth. "Could a man or woman do any more," he thought, "than this wild doe—or do it more nobly or freely? I am a hunter, it's true. I kill to eat. But I'm a man, too, not a beast. I need not always kill."

"Lady," he said, "animal or not, your words have touched my rough, hunter's heart. Though I've never released a single creature from my snares before, today both you and your lord shall go free!"

Leaving his spear, he approached the stag. Stooping down, he pulled open the sharp noose with his calloused hands. "Arise, Great Stag," said the hunter, "and go freely with your doe! She has saved you both today."

The great stag rose painfully. He leaned against the doe's slender shoulder for support. "Friend," he said, "virtue is a priceless jewel and our only refuge in times of danger and trial. You have done a good deed this day. Let me repay you." And, lowering his head, he dug in the earth with a golden antler, unearthing a priceless gem. "Take this jewel," he said, "and live in peace. May it sustain you and your family through all difficult times to come. And may it help you, kind hunter, never to have to kill again!"

And then the great stag turned and, with the brave and faithful doe beside him, limped off, disappearing back into the forest again.

The hunter watched them go. Soon he stood alone beneath the great trees, the topmost branches tossing, the leaves fluttering and turning in the wind. He could hear wild forest birds singing freely all around. In his hands he held a jewel worth a fortune.

Gathering up his spear and snare, he left that forest with a free man's swinging stride, resolved never to kill another living thing.

So you see, the power of even one good deed can hardly be measured.

The Hare's Sacrifice

Once
the Buddha was born

as a tender-hearted hare. He lived in a large forest and had joined together with an otter, a monkey, and a fox, in order to keep religious vows. The four animals decided that once a month they would hold a fast day and give the food they might have eaten on that day to someone hungrier than themselves.

A month goes by quickly in a forest. The trees bend and shift in the wind; the clouds drift slowly across the sun, and race at night across the moon; the clear streams rush on, carrying leaves and twigs and bugs down over the rocks and flow on, heaven knows where. Soon, another fast day had arrived.

"I will be good," thought the otter to himself, scratching his stomach and fluffing up his wet fur. Slipping into the water, he swam across the shining lake. There, on the other shore, he found a fisherman's camp. Seven fish lay on the grass, strung together on a slender stick. "Is anyone here?" called the otter quietly. "Well, these fish must have gotten lost," he decided, and taking the stick firmly in his teeth, he reentered the water and swam home. "Someone will have a fine feast," he thought somewhat sadly. "But, alas, it's not going to be me!" And feeling very righteous, he sat down in the sun to rest.

The monkey too, swinging in the trees, thought of the fast and resolved to be good. He would give his own meal to another. Hunting around, he found beautiful bananas and mangoes. "Why couldn't I have found these yesterday?" he couldn't help but think. "Well, today they shall be given to another." And, setting them aside, he too rested in his tree, feeling very righteous indeed.

Now the fox was trotting along, his sharp nose to the wind. Catching the scent of cooked foods, he bounded through the bushes until he came to a farmer's hut. "Ho, ho!" he thought to himself. "What, no one around? Why, someone's left a pot of yoghurt on the ground and a bit of bread baking on a spit!" Slipping his head through the cord attached to the pot and taking the spit of bread between his teeth, he trotted off, the plume of his tail waving with delight as he thought of the fine meal that lay ahead. He had not gone far when he remembered the fast day. His tail drooped. "Oh well, someone is going to eat well," he said, and then, recovering his spirits, he trotted on, feeling very righteous indeed.

But the hare thought and thought. "Today is the fast day. I'm tired of giving carrots and cabbages and potatoes and such things. What kind of sacrifice is it for me to offer what already grows so freely in the ground? No, today I am of a mind to achieve some greater goal, to make a sacrifice that really shows how I feel. Aha!" cried the hare, leaping up, "I have it. Today I shall offer my own body to someone in need."

Up in the heavens, Shakra's marble throne grew hot, a sign that, somewhere on earth, someone was preparing to achieve a noble deed. "Ah," thought the king of the gods, "a little hare is about to take a big leap. I shall test him." In less than an instant, the high god appeared in the little hare's forest. Taking the form of an old beggar, he hobbled off, leaning on a staff, to where the otter was resting by the lake shore.

"Friend," said the old beggar, extending a trembling hand, "can you spare a little food for me?"

"Of course," said the otter, "sit down." Running to his den, he dragged out five of the fish and lay them at the beggar's calloused feet. "Eat well," said the otter.

"Thank you," said the beggar, "for your kindness. I may be back for these." And hobbling off, he left the astonished otter alone by the shore once again.

Next, he came to the monkey. "Have you some food for a weary traveler?" he asked, in an exhausted voice.

"Of course, sit down," said the monkey, who scampered up his tree and returned with several bananas and a mango. "Eat," he said. "Enjoy. These are fresh and ripe."

"Thank you," said Shakra, rising to his feet, "I may be back for these." Striding off, he left the monkey scratching his head in confusion.

Next, he approached the fox. "Help me," he cried. "I am old and very hungry. Have you any food?"

"Of course," yelped the fox. "I've got just the thing." Racing off, he returned with the pot of yoghurt and the spit of bread. He threw himself down, grinning and panting, delighted with his goodness. But, to his amazement, the old man rose and marched off into the twilight, saying "Thank you, I may be back!"

Then the god, Shakra, came to the little hare just as the moon was rising. "Friend," he groaned, "I have not eaten for many days. The roads have been hard and I am faint. Have you anything at all that I might eat?"

"Yes," said the hare, "please seat yourself and be patient, for tonight you shall have such a meal as I have never offered before!" Then, gathering leaves and twigs he started a small blaze on the rocks of the forest floor. When the fire was hot and burning fiercely, the little hare shook himself to save any fleas that might be living in his coat. Then, leaping high, he jumped straight into the flames! But what was this? The fire was cool! It was like ice! Not a hair or pore of his body was even singed!

"Come out from the flames, brave little hare," said a noble voice. And leaping out from the fire once again, the little hare found himself facing one of the radiant gods. It was Shakra himself! The old beggar had vanished.

"What! What has happened?" exclaimed the astonished hare.

"You are the great event that has happened," answered Shakra, the king of the gods. "You shall be remembered for this for an entire eon. Look!" And reaching upward, he drew the hare's picture, with his finger, on the shining disk of the moon. "There," he said, "your sacrifice will be remembered for as long as the moon shall still shine in the sky. Now, come with me for a while, little hare," said the king of the gods with a bow. "Let me show you my home." Bending down, the mighty god gently lifted the little, wide-eyed hare up into his arms. Then, soaring upward, they disappeared together beyond the bright sparks rising from the fire.

The forest became very still. The flames of the fire died down. A glowing log popped, shooting up a last burst of sparks. The sparks whirled up and up, drifting higher and higher, until they too disappeared, lost at last against the brilliance of the moon and stars.

After that, the three friends, the otter, the monkey and the fox, lived on in harmony. Encouraging each other, they kept their vows. Seated together in the forest, they would look up at the full moon and remember with amazement the day that the king of the gods himself had come to test them. And they would recall their friend the little hare and his sacrifice.

All that was long, long ago. But the hare-in-the-moon

still shines just as brightly in the night sky as he did when Shakra first put him up there—a sign for all to see that compassion is the light that illumines our darkness.

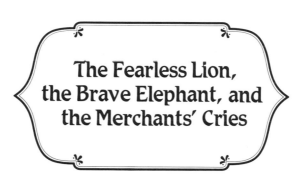

The Fearless Lion,
the Brave Elephant, and
the Merchants' Cries

Once

the Buddha was born

as a fearless and powerful lion. He lived on a large island. There he freely roamed the jungles and, with his sharp teeth and claws, took whatever prey he chose.

This lion had one close friend—a great bull elephant. These two powerful animals often got together to talk. Sometimes they even traveled together, exploring the caves, forests, mountains, and shorelines of their home. They respected each other deeply. Though the lion was a hunter, an eater of flesh, and the tusked elephant fed only on grasses and fruits, they got along well. The lion's snarling, coughing roar and the elephant's bold trumpeting both sounded the same fearless note.

One day the lion and the elephant were walking at the jungle's edge, not far from the seashore. The lion lifted his heavy, golden-maned head and sniffed the sharp, salty air. He listened to the gulls crying shrilly among the breakers. Suddenly he heard desperate cries, the terror-stricken screams of men who are facing violent death.

With a roar, the lion leapt forward, his heart racing fiercely, and called for his friend the elephant to follow. The lion raced along the sandy beach, his large paws kicking up clouds of shining sand. The elephant raced along behind him, maddened too by the agonizing cries. They reached a final ridge overlooking the breakers and the sea. There, below them, a group of shipwrecked merchants ran frantically like herded sheep. A monstrous serpent had come up out of the sea surrounding them with the glittering loops of its gigantic coils. The serpent's sharp scales and cold green eyes glistened; its curved fangs dripped a pale venom.

The lion and the elephant looked at each other. "We'll help!" they cried with one voice. The lion leaped upon the elephant's broad, domed head. Steadying himself with his claws, he lashed his tail and roared. The elephant, trumpeting mightily, charged, carrying them together into battle. The serpent looked up and, with a long, murderous hiss, released the merchants. Its head rose into the air. Drawing itself coil upon coil up out of the foaming, salty sea, it slid angrily forward along the sandy beach toward the oncoming lion and elephant.

The battle was terrible and bloody. The lion's roaring, the elephant's trumpeting, and the serpent's hissing drowned out even the sounds of the ocean. The merchants ran in terror into the jungle and threw themselves down on the ground, covering their ears with their hands. It was as if the world was coming to an end. Great clouds of blinding sand were thrown up whirling into the sky, and nothing, not even the sun, could be seen.

Several hours later all sounds of battle ceased and the air cleared. Only the murmuring ocean rolled in, sounding above the screeching of the gulls. The merchants peered out fearfully from among the trees.

There lay the long body of the serpent, bloody now and crushed; its pale belly was up, gleaming in the sun; its once bright, hard scales were dull and torn. It was dead. There, too, lay the two fearless friends, the great lion and the mighty elephant, alive, but dying. The serpent's venom had done its deadly work.

Later, the merchants built a great pyre on the beach and on it, with all honors, they placed the body of the two noble beasts, the elephant and the lion. They wondered why

those two wild animals had saved them. They wondered, "Why did two such powerful beasts give up their own lives for us?"

And still we wonder today. For even if one spoke for a thousand years with a thousand mouths, or wrote in a thousand books with one thousand hands, one could still never begin to explain or exhaust the mystery of compassion.

The Banyan Deer

Once

the Buddha was born

as a Banyan deer. When he was grown, he became the leader of the herd. He guided his deer with care and brought them to the safety of a secluded forest. There they dwelt in ease for several years. Grazing in the meadows and resting among the giant trees, it seemed that they had truly found peace and contentment at last.

But all things change. In time, a new king came into power over the land. And this king's favorite pastime was, unfortunately, hunting. He would mount his horse and, rousing his men just as the sun was breaking over the hills, lead them on a furious chase through the mountains and forests. Shooting his arrows madly, the king always raced in the very forefront and would not leave off his sport until the sun was setting, red as blood. By then, the wagons which followed behind him were filled with the carcasses of deer and bear, rabbit and boar, and sometimes even panther and lion. "Hunting," thought the king to himself, as he rode ahead of the creaking wagons, "is a noble sport. It keeps rulers fit and warlike. Besides, there is nothing like feasting on red meat!" And he was happy.

But his subjects were not. The courtiers were exhausted. After days and days of hunting, all other entertainments had ceased. Their minds became coarse and dark. They were moody and sullen. "Enough killing," some said. "Isn't there anything more to life?" The merchants and farmers felt even worse. Their fields were being ruined and many of their shops had closed. Everyone was so busy hunting that their own livelihoods were in danger. Many of them had been forced to ride along on the hunt to drive the frightened animals out of the thickets and load the wagons for the long ride home. They had had enough!

A meeting was called and eventually the poorest of the king's subjects devised a plan. "We can no longer afford to keep up this new king's bloody pace. Rather than running all over, chasing wild beasts here and there, wasting time and ruining crops, let's build a stockade and trap a whole herd or two of deer within it. Then, whenever the king wants to go hunting, he can go to this one place and shoot to his heart's content. If it's meat he wants, then it's meat he'll get," they laughed, "but not from our flesh!"

Now, when the king heard about the stockade and the grievances of his people, he grew thoughtful. Feasting and sport were one thing, endangering the welfare of his state was another. He had never meant to be a burden to his subjects. With a sigh, he agreed to hunt from the walls of the stockade, rather than go riding wildly through the countryside.

A huge wooden stockade was built in a deep, green forest. And two herds of terrified deer were driven within its walls by shouting men. The gates were closed and the delicate animals charged and wheeled in frantic circles, seeking some exit, some way out. But there was none. At last, exhausted and trembling, they stood with dark, frightened eyes, awaiting their fate. The men left laughing to tell the king of their success, relieved that their own problems were finally over. "Now we can get back to business," they said happily. One of the herds they had captured was the herd of the Banyan deer.

Locked within the stockade, the Banyan deer tried to calm his frightened herd. Sunlight played on his many-

branched antlers. His black eyes shone and his muzzle was wet. "The clear blue sky is still overhead and green grass grows at our feet," he said. "Let us not give up. Where there is life, there is still hope. I will find a way." And he tried to keep up their spirits and ease their fears.

Soon the king arrived to view the captured herds. "Ah," he exclaimed, "two fine herds of deer." His eyes found the leaders of each herd. "Why, the leaders of both herds are magnificent animals," he announced. "No one is to shoot them. They shall live unharmed." Then, drawing his own bow, he quickly shot his arrows into the milling herds, felling enough deer for the palace kitchens in just a few minutes. Again the two herds became frantic. Racing wildly, they injured each other in their efforts to escape the deadly arrows.

And so it went. Every few days, the king and his courtiers would return. And every few days, more of the gentle deer were killed. But many of the deer were also injured by the horns and hoofs of the others as they ran; many hurt themselves in their wild efforts to escape and many others were wounded by the flying arrows.

The king of the Banyan deer met with the leader of the other herd. "Brother," he said, shaking his antlered head, "we are trapped. I've tried every way out, but all are barred. The pain our subjects suffer in this death trap is horrible! They are getting hurt just trying to escape and wild arrows are wounding many others as well. Let us arrange a lottery. Every deer must pick a straw. The deer who draws the shortest, one day from your herd and one day from mine, must go willingly and alone to the huntsmen. In this way, hard as it is, we shall at least be able to reduce the injuries and pain." And the leader of the other herd agreed.

So, when the king and his courtiers next arrived at the stockade, they found a deer standing directly below them, shaking, but with head held high. "What is this?" thought the king. "Ah, I see! I see! These are noble deer indeed! They have chosen to come by lot rather than cause all the deer to suffer the dangers of our hunt." A heaviness descended on the king's heart. What was it? He did not know. Nodding to his courtiers, he himself set down his bow. "Food is needed, but no more unnecessary killing. We will keep to the deer's own terms," he announced. "From now on, only shoot the deer who waits directly below." And with these orders, he left the wall of the stockade, mounted his horse, and rode back slowly to the palace.

"What's bothering the king?" wondered the courtiers, watching him ride off. At last they shrugged and went on with their job.

That night, the king still brooded and pondered. "What is it," he asked himself, "that weighs on me so? Is something lacking from my rule?" He slept fitfully, and a radiant deer paced through his dreams.

One day, the lot fell on a doe of the other deer's herd. Because she was carrying an unborn fawn, she went to her king and asked that she be allowed to live until her fawn was born. Then she would go willingly to the huntsmen, she said. But her king said no. Who, after all, would take her place? The lot was impartial and her turn had come. There could be no exceptions. Those were the rules.

In desperation she ran to the Banyan deer, who was sitting He sat beneath a shade tree, watching his herd. She fell on her knees before him and begged for his aid. He listened quietly, watching her face all the while with wide and gentle eyes. "Rise," he said at last. "Your words are right. You shall be freed from the lottery until your fawn is grown."

"But," she said, "who will take my place?"

"Don't worry," replied the Banyan deer, "I will take care of that."

Too overjoyed for more words, she bowed gratefully

to the deer king and bounded away in relief.

The deer king rose to his feet. He would not ask another to take the place of the doe he had just spared. He had freed her, so he would take her place. How could he ask that of another?

He walked calmly, in great dignity, through his browsing herd. They watched him as he moved among them. His curving antlers and strong shoulders, his shining eyes and sharp, black hoofs, all reassured and comforted them. Never had their deer king let them down. If there was a way, he would find it. Never had he lost his herd to the many dangers they had already faced; never had he abandoned any of them. Never had he lorded it over them either. He was a king, indeed, and his whole herd took comfort in his presence.

The courtiers were waiting with their bows drawn atop the stockade. Their king had not come with them this day. When they saw the Banyan deer approach they shouted together, "King of the Banyan deer! Why have you come to the place of slaughter? Don't you know that our king has freed you?"

"I know," replied the Banyan deer, "but I have come so that two others don't have to die. Now shoot! You have your work and I have mine."

But the amazed courtiers did not shoot. Rather, putting down their bows, they sent a message at once to the king. "Your majesty, come with all speed," it read. "A strange event awaits you at the stockade." Mounting his horse, the king rode like the wind, his robes streaming behind him.

"What is it?" he said, descending from his horse.

"Look," they cried. "It is the Banyan deer."

The king hurried up the rough wooden steps. At last, he stood at the top, looking down over the wall.

There stood the deer king. Human king and deer king

looked at each other.

"Banyan deer," said the king of men, "now I recognize you! It is you I have seen moving phantom-like through my dream forests. Tell me, why have you come? You know that I have already freed you from the hunt."

"Great king," said the Banyan deer, "who of us is free if our people suffer? Today a doe with fawn asked for my aid. The lottery had fallen on her. Now I shall take her place. This is my right and my duty as king."

A weight rolled from the king's own heart. "Noble Banyan deer," he said, "you are right! A king must care for the least of his subjects. Go free, now, brave Deer King, you and your whole herd. None of you shall be hunted again. This is my gift to you. It is a teacher's fee for the lesson you have taught me. Go now, and live in peace."

"Great king," said the Banyan deer, "it is a noble gift. But I cannot go. I must speak further. Will you listen?"

"Certainly, Noble Deer. Speak and I will listen."

"What, Great King," now asked the Banyan deer, "of the other herd? My own herd's safety will only expose them to greater danger, will it not?"

"Yes," said the king of men, reflecting for a moment. "Yes, it will."

"Then," said the Banyan deer, "I cannot leave."

"What! Would you risk your own and your herd's freedom for them?" asked the king in surprise.

"Yes," said the Banyan deer, "I would. Think of their anguish, Great King, and let them go free."

The king of men paused, momentarily lost in thought. Then he lifted his head and smiled. "All right," he said, "your courage and compassion have moved me. They too shall go free. Tell me, noble deer, are you now at peace?"

"No, Great King," said the Banyan deer, "I am not. I am thinking of all the other wild and hunted creatures. All my life I have lived, like them, surrounded by danger and

fear. Their sufferings have been my own. So now, I cannot be truly at peace unless they are free, too."

"I see," said the king of men. Then again, after a brief pause, he went on. "So be it. They too are freed. Never again shall I allow any wild creature to be hunted or slain in all my realm. There, Noble One," he added, "are you now at peace?"

"No, Great King," said the Banyan deer, "I am not. What, my Lord, of the defenseless birds? A net of danger still surrounds them. Stones and arrows greet them wherever they fly. Will you not release them, too?"

"Yes!" exclaimed the king, "Yes, I will! They shall fly freely from this day on throughout my realm. No one shall hunt them ever again. We shall let them soar the skies and build their nests in peace. There," he said, "are you satisfied? Are you now at peace?"

"Great King," replied the Banyan deer, "think for a moment of the fish. They swim the cool lakes, rivers, and streams of your land. Yet, even as we stand here speaking, your nets, hooks, and fish spears are poised over them, ready to strike. If I do not now speak for these silent ones, who ever will? Will you not spare them as well?"

"Yes, Noble Being," said the king of men at last, tears trickling down his cheeks. "Yes, I will. Now, all of you courtiers and attendants, hear my words. This is my proclamation. See that it is posted throughout the land. From this day forth, all beings in my realm shall be freed from slaughter. Never again shall any be hunted, trapped, or killed. This is my lasting decree. Now, tell me, Noble One," he said, turning to the Banyan deer again, "are you at peace?"

The Banyan deer looked up. A flock of small birds flew swiftly through the blue sky. All around him the gentle deer grazed quietly on green grass. "Yes," he said, "Now I am at peace!" And bounding high into the air, he leapt like a fawn—he leapt for joy, sheer joy. He had saved them all!

Then, thanking the king, he gathered his herd and led them safely back to their old forest home.

Later, the king of men erected a stone pillar at the spot where the Banyan deer had leapt for joy. The figure of a deer was carved on it, encircled with these words, "Never Cease To Care." Then he too, caring for all living things, lived on in peace and freedom for many, many years.

King Sivi

Once
there was

a kind king. He was wealthy and respected and his kingdom was at peace. But he was not content. He was not happy. Sitting at the window of his throne room, he looked out over the well-trimmed lawns and tree-lined streets of his city, and out over the green fields of his land. He sighed. "I would like to really give," he said. "Life is short; even the virtuous gods do not live forever. Yet, though I have had my successes, I have not really given of myself." Now this was not exactly true. He had given his time, energy, and courage to the welfare of his country. He had listened patiently and kindly to the daily cares and problems of his people and had ruled them wisely. He had, in short, been a good king. But perhaps when one is good one hardly knows it oneself. At least that is how it seems to have been with this good King Sivi.

Shakra, king of the gods, heard this lament and thought to himself, "This King Sivi has led a good life so far. The gates of the heavens will certainly open to him when his years on earth are over. Yet he is now calling for a decisive test. The strong languish without challenge and, in the fields of goodness, Sivi is strong. Why, his many good deeds on earth have already built him extensive palaces and gardens here among us in which he will dwell for many thousands of earthly years. Still, a test is now in order. Aha," exclaimed Shakra, "I have it!"

Suddenly the king of the gods transformed himself. Where but a moment before—a moment, that is, by heavenly reckoning, which could equal two, or even three, earthly weeks—he had sat resplendent on his throne, wearing his robes and jeweled crown, there now perched two birds. One was a gentle, gray-eyed dove, which called in a soft, sweet melodious voice. The other was a fierce hawk, with yellow eyes, talons like knives, and a cruel, curved beak. The hawk ruffled his feathers and glared at the bright godly light of the upper realms. The dove cooed softly and, flapping her wings, darted down through the clouds. Faster and faster and faster raced the little shining dove. Down and down and down. And faster and faster and faster flew the golden-eyed hawk after her. Turning and twisting, they dove down towards the green earth and the marble palaces of King Sivi.

Soon the dove forgot that she had ever been just a thought in the mind of a god. The hawk too no longer remembered that he was but a god's dream. Now he flew after the little dove in deadly earnest, striving only to grasp the dove in his talons and to tear and devour her at last. So the little, gentle dove flew on in increasing terror as the moments of their deadly race sped by.

The dove spied an open window and, near exhaustion, sped through it. There sat King Sivi on his gold and sandalwood throne. The terrified dove darted to the king's side and perched, shaking, on the carved arm of his throne. "What is it, little bird?" asked the king in surprise. "What frightens you so? Can I help?"

"Oh, Lord," panted the dove, "a fierce hawk is after me. He wants to take my life."

"Don't worry. I will save you," said the king kindly. "I won't let him take you."

At that very moment, the hawk burst into the room. Drawing his wings together he swiftly perched upon the

throne's other arm and saluted the king. "Great King," he said, "my lawful prey sits by you. I am weary with the chase. Give me the dove and I will depart in peace."

"I cannot give the dove to you," said the king. "I have promised her my protection."

"That is all very well," said the hawk, "but what of my rights? I am a hunting bird. Doves are my food. You have robbed me of what is lawfully mine and, without food, I shall starve this very night."

"Well, I can't let you starve," said the king with concern. "I'll give you some other food. Tell me what you need."

"I need fresh meat in order to live," said the hawk. "Could you really kill another creature just to feed me? Somehow I don't think so. Come," he said at last, "give me the dove. It's the simplest way."

"It's true!" thought the king, "I couldn't kill some other creature in order to supply him with food. He's right. That would be no solution at all! Yet, I can't let him have the dove. He will kill her. But if I don't let him have her he himself shall die. What right have I to let even a hawk starve in my presence? As a living creature with a place in the scheme of things, he also deserves my help." The king sat silently, tugging at his beard. Then, all at once, he rose to his feet. "I have it!" he announced.

"Fierce hawk," he said, "I have a plan. You shall be fed, the dove shall remain free, and no other creature need be killed."

"What is your plan?" asked the hawk suspiciously.

"It's simple," said the king. "I will give you a piece of my own flesh. As it shall weigh exactly as much as the dove's body, you will lose nothing by the bargain. Will you agree to this?"

"Yes," said the hawk, "I will. As long as the piece you give me weighs exactly as much as the dove, I shall be satisfied."

"Good! You have my word."

A golden scale was brought from the treasury and set before the throne. The little dove was placed in one of the scale's hanging trays. A silver perch was brought for the hawk and a little, smooth golden dish was set before him. Then, the weeping noblewomen were directed to leave the room. The king's physicians and courtiers argued with him. They begged him, in the name of reason, to stop. But the king was resolved. "I will give what I can," he said. "After all, how much can a little bird weigh?"

A sharp knife with an inlaid handle was brought in on an embroidered cushion. The room grew quiet. King Sivi took up the knife. Then, in terrible silence, he sliced a piece of flesh from the muscle of his thigh and placed it on the scale. Bright blood ran down his leg but not a single groan escaped his lips. He watched the pointer. But the scale did not move! The dove's side of the balance did not rise at all! Unflinchingly, the king cut more flesh from his thigh. But again, the golden scale would not rise. Unhesitatingly, he cut and cut and cut. He cut till both thighs were like sticks. Then he cut the flesh from his left arm. But still the scale would not rise. Too weak to cut any more, he dropped the knife and had his whole body placed in the now bloody scale.

"Enough!" cried the hawk and dove together with a single voice. The chamber was lit with a golden light. Both birds were gone! In the center of the room hovered Shakra, king of the shining gods. And beside him, standing firmly on the polished floor, stood King Sivi, whole and completely unharmed.

"Noble King," said the god, "you have been tested as few have ever been tested. And you have passed nobly. For this, you shall live for many years and your kingdom shall be at peace. Later, you shall reside near me, in the highest heavens, for many thousands of years before returning to

this earth. Be well, O King, for today you have done well, indeed." And Shakra, as is his way, vanished, leaving not a trace.

Then the people of the kingdom came running to the king. They embraced him, crying with joy. And everything came to pass as Shakra had announced. There was peace and harmony for many, many years.

Eventually, King Sivi did go to live among the gods. But often, seated in splendor at the window of his shining palace, he would look with love out over the earth and all its creatures. He would think, too, with joy of the day to come when he would be back on the earth again. What contentment, after all, can a kindly heart have in heaven?

So, in time, King Sivi returned, as you shall see.

The Hungry
Tigress

Once,
long, long ago,

the Buddha came to life as a noble prince named Mahasattva, in a land where the country of Nepal exists today. One day, when he was grown, he went walking in a wild forest with his two older brothers. The land was dry and the leaves brittle. The sky seemed alight with flames.

Suddenly, they saw a tigress. The brothers turned to flee, but the tigress stumbled and fell. She was starving and desperate and her two cubs were starving, too. She eyed her cubs miserably and, in that dark glance, the prince sensed long months of hunger and pain. He saw, too, that unless she had food soon she might even be driven to devour her own cubs. He was moved by compassion for the hardness of their life. "What, after all, is this life for?" he thought.

Stepping forward, he removed his outer garments and lay down before her. Tearing his skin with a stone, he let the starving tigress smell the blood. Mahasattva's brothers fled.

Hungrily, the tigress devoured the prince's body and chewed the bones. She and her cubs lived on, and for many years the forest was filled with a golden light.

Centuries later, a mighty king raised a pillar of carved stone on this spot and pilgrims still go there to make offerings even today.

Deeds of Compassion live on forever.

Leaving Home

Two thousand
five hundred years ago,

the Buddha was born as a prince in the foothills of the Himalayan mountains—the highest peaks on this earth. When he was born, his father received a prophecy that his son would either become a great king or, if he became aware of life's sufferings, he would leave home and enter the mountains. There, he would undergo many painful trials and difficulties, but he would, in the end, awaken to the highest Truth. Moved by compassion, he would become a teacher to gods, beasts, and men.

The child's father, the King Suddhodhana, wanted to protect his son from hardship. He didn't want him to leave home or to suffer. And so, he tried to keep his child from even the sight of sickness, old age, or death.

He named the boy Siddhartha ("He Whose Wishes Are Fulfilled") and used all the power at his command to try to make sure that the boy's life was always happy and pleasant.

And, for a number of years, it seemed that he might, in fact, succeed. Young Siddhartha played happily in beautiful gardens. During the fierce heat of the Indian summers, he roamed the cool halls of marble palaces. Anything he wanted was his. His playmates and friends adored him. Loving attendants surrounded him. He grew strong and took well to a king's education. As he grew older, he learned the sciences, arts, and the skills of a warrior and ruler. The whole kingdom was pleased. They had a good king, and a promising, worthy heir.

But Siddhartha, "He Whose Wishes Are Fulfilled," was himself not truly happy. He began to see what his father no longer could. He saw the hooded cobras hunting frogs and mice in the gardens and was moved to pity. He saw the terrified doves fleeing the keen-eyed hawks. He saw the gentle deer being carried to the palace limply slung on the hunter's poles. He noticed all the many little fleeting sadnesses of his friends, such as when they lost at a footrace or did not receive the gift on which their hearts had been set. He tried, in vain, to remember the face of the mother he had never seen.

Little by little, these impressions piled up within him like dry twigs that a spark might ignite.

One day, though he had married and lived in luxury, the thought struck him that he had never really seen the world of ordinary men and women. He went to his charioteer. "Take me, Channa, into the towns," he said. "I want to see my subjects; I want to see how they really live."

"Very good, sire," said Channa, the charioteer. "Let us go tomorrow. I will make the necessary arrangements."

And the prince was content.

The king, Siddhartha's father, had been dreading this moment for many years. Channa now went to the king and told him that the time had come—Siddhartha wanted to leave the palace estate and enter the world. "No!" exclaimed the king. "Prophecy or no, I shall not lose him! We shall keep him from knowledge of life's pain for a few years yet. There will always be Truth to seek," he added, distressed. "Let him seek it later, after he has been a king. He is my only son!"

The king called in the captain of the guards. "Go to the villages," he said, "and make sure that no beggars, no old, and no sick persons are out on the streets. Perfume the roads, hang wreaths of flowers, and, above all, make sure

that no funerals are held! These are my commands. See to it that they are fulfilled!"

"Yes, your Majesty," said the captain of the guards. Bowing, he withdrew from the throne room and set out at once with a company of armed men.

All was done exactly as the king had ordered. Yet, the king remained anxious. He paced the polished stone corridors of the palace, glancing out at the silent stars and waxing moon.

The sun rose; the day broke. Siddhartha and Channa set off for the town. The horses raced easily along the hard, dirt road. Birds sang and soared among the trees. White clouds drifted slowly high overhead. A cool breeze blew and the mountains, rising behind them, glowed in the early light. Soon, they arrived at the town. It was beautiful. Flowers hung everywhere. Crowds cheered the prince's arrival. Children laughed; happy couples strolled arm in arm. "Ah," thought the prince to himself, "so, this is life! Why have I been sad? These people are happy. Now I can return to the palace and live my own life without concern."

But what was this? Suddenly, a wrinkled and toothless old man, bent and twisted with years, tottered out from the crowd. For a few minutes he stood blinking blindly and most pitifully in the bright sunlight. Then he was gone! The horses lay back their ears and neighed shrilly, in terror. Rearing up, they tried to back away. The prince leaped from the chariot and grabbed their bridles. "Channa, what was that?" he cried. "Was that a man or was that some other kind of creature?"

"Noble Prince," replied Channa, "that was indeed a man, even as you and I. He was simply an old, old man, sire."

The prince was confused. "Tell me Channa," he asked, "do all men become like this? Do all men become old?"

"Not only men," replied Channa, for the gods had

loosened his tongue, "but all creatures on this earth become old, my Prince."

Shaken, the prince remounted the chariot. "Turn the horses around and let us return," he said. "Here indeed is a bitter truth, reason enough to spill an ocean of tears." Channa turned the horses and they rode back, dispirited, to the palace once again.

But the next morning the prince again rose with the sun. Waking Channa, he said, "Whatever lies ahead must, after all, be faced. Let us face it bravely. We shall return to the town. It is not yet over."

Once again, the horses raced along the road; once again, the fine breezes blew. Yesterday now seemed like a nightmare which daylight dissolves. "What is yesterday," said Channa happily to the prince as they rode on together, "but a dream already long gone by?" And it seemed to be true. Everything was beautiful. The trembling leaves, the rising light, the immense mountains, the billowing clouds, the bright flowers swaying by the roadside. All were fresh and new again. How could there be pain or sadness in such a world?

Soon they entered the town. Once more the crowds cheered and smiled. But still, the prince yearned to know the truth. The crowds seemed to part before him, and a sick man tottered from the curb. He was thin, sweaty, and disheveled. His eyes were red and weepy. He coughed and almost fell. The happy people recoiled in alarm. Covering their mouths, they backed quickly away. "What is that?" cried the prince. "Channa! What has happened to that man?"

"He is sick," said Channa. "His elements are disordered; he is feverish and tormented."

"Was he born like this?" asked the prince.

"No," said Channa. "He was probably born as sound as you or I."

"Can we all become sick then?" asked the prince.

"Yes," replied Channa, again impelled by the ever-watchful gods to speak the truth, "we can."

"Turn the horses round," exclaimed the prince in dismay. "With old age on one hand and sickness on the other, my interest in festivities is gone."

And, once again, they traveled back in silence to the palace through the burning midday heat.

Cool night fell at last. But, though the stars shone and sparkled overhead, the prince could take no delight in them. All night long he lay feverishly, tossing with the thought of old age and sickness. It was as if a blaze had begun burning within him.

Oh, but when the sun rose over the mountains, hope again awoke in the prince's heart. "Let what is to come, come," he thought. "Whatever it is, I can meet it; I can find a way through." For he was more certain than ever that this was not yet the end, not yet the end at all, of the road he was destined to travel.

So once again Siddhartha and Channa set off toward the town.

How innocent and fresh the town looked that morning! Little flocks of white pigeons wheeled among the bright buildings and perched, cooing, beneath the roof eaves. Children chased brightly painted balls, skipped, and sang old rhyming songs. Smiling couples strolled together, talking and laughing.

But what were those cries? That wailing and weeping? "Channa," exclaimed the prince, "stop the horses! What is happening? Tell me, what is it?"

"It is a funeral, sire," said Channa with a shiver. "It marks a death."

But the prince did not understand. Running ahead, he came to the source of the keening cries. "Channa," he called, "why does that one not move? Why does he not awake and arise?"

"He is dead, my lord," said Channa unhappily, his own voice giving form to the thoughts of the gods.

"What! What is that you say?" cried the prince in alarm. "What do you mean, 'He is dead'?"

"His life is over, Lord," said Channa. "There will be no more action or movement, no more laughter or tears for him."

"No more movement? No more life?" asked the astonished prince.

"No, my lord," continued Channa, still moved by the gods. "For him there will be no more sight or smell or sound or thought, no more hopes or dreams. His days are done; it is over. His friends and relations may weep all they want, still, they will not see him again."

"Surely," asked the prince with an awful sense of foreboding, "that does not happen to everyone?"

Channa turned away. But again the far-seeing gods loosened his tongue so that he spoke the bitter truth. "Sire, it does. It happens to everyone, to everything, to all."

"To all?" repeated the prince as if struck.

"Yes, all," said Channa, his own eyes filling with tears.

The funeral procession was gone. Once again, the smiling crowds gathered.

"Is this the end?" asked the prince in disbelief. "Is this, after all, the end I have sought?"

"I do not know, sire," said Channa now that the gods were gone from him. "I do not know at all!"

"No, brave Prince," said a firm voice behind him. "This is not yet the end. It is not yet the end at all." Turning, the prince saw a hermit, a mysterious recluse of the mountains, leaning on a wooden staff. "No," the recluse went on, "it is not the end. Rather, it is where we begin. Walk on, young prince, walk on! The more you climb these moun-

tains the higher they get. You are still in the foothills. Seek the heights, Siddhartha, the heights! There your wishes will indeed be fulfilled." And then the hermit was gone!

Mounting his chariot as if in a dream, the prince and Channa rode back in silence to the palace once again. Words now arose in the prince's mind, sounding over and over with the rhythm of the horses's hoofs: "Now is the time to enter the mountains! Now is the time to seek the great heights!"

Parrots, tigers, oxen, monkeys, rabbits, lions, quails, and deer; princes, sages, kings, warriors, merchants, and poor, simple men seemed to be racing alongside the chariot keeping pace with him. All these memories and images of Siddhartha's own long-forgotten past now cried out together to him with a single voice, "To the mountains! To the peaks at last!"

Like a flood, a river of hope and courage surged through the prince's heart. Standing firmly in the rocking chariot, he saw the mountains looming closer and closer, rising higher and higher as the horses sped on.

So now, the long-protected prince, Siddhartha, was about to set out on the path of his own ripening destiny. He was indeed about to leave his father's home.

Enlightenment

At the age
of twenty-nine,

the prince of the Shakya Clan, Siddhartha Gautama, saw for the first time: an old man, a sick man, a dead man, and a hermit or monk. Then a great fire flared up within him and he had no more comfort or peace.

One night, just a few days after his meeting with the mysterious hermit, he slipped quietly out of the palace, mounted his horse, and entered the forest. He rode for hours. Just before dawn he arrived at the river boundary of his father's kingdom. The sky was like a purple robe bordered with fire. A single, silver star shone, and a pale, golden crescent moon hung above the trees. He drew his sword and with one stroke severed his long hair and jeweled topknot. Then, trading clothes with a poor hunter who was passing by, and bidding his horse Kanthaka farewell, he crossed the river and disappeared into the forests and mountains. There, as had been prophesied at his birth, he took up, for truth's sake, a life of hardship and unrelenting exertion.

He sought out the best teachers and, quickly attaining what they had to offer, moved on again, this time to the more desperate path of extreme asceticism, thinking that perhaps here lay the means for triumphing over birth, old age, sickness, and death.

And he continued to drive himself mercilessly along this desperate and painful course for six agonizing years. At last, starved beyond recognition, he collapsed, more a skeleton wound with sinews and veins than a living man.

His great effort had seemingly failed. For all his willful suffering, he had not been able to achieve the enlightenment for which he deeply yearned. As he lay there, in despair, the memory of a certain festival, years earlier, flashed through his mind. He had been just a child then. Seated quietly under a rose-apple tree he had been watching his father and all the nobles and poor men alike plowing the earth together. All at once he had become aware of the earth, breaking open in even wavelike furrows; the heat shimmering up off the freshly opened soil and shining on the sweat-slick brows and straining bodies of men and oxen alike; the sun, continuously flashing off thc gilded traces and horns of the oxen; the senseless plodding rhythm of hooves and cowbells rolling in a solemn sealike way beneath the shriller shouts of the men, and the remorseless, whirring cries of the birds as they dove to peck at and devour the billowing hordes of insects, blind, glistening grubs, cut worms, and broken bodies of mice, which the men, oxen and plows left in their wake.

How that terrible laboring and suffering, that unheeded and awful devouring and dying had shocked and pained him. "What kind of world is this?" he had thought, with the enormous, solemn grief of a sensitive child. The hot fields shimmered before him as he sat, unmoving and stricken, on his cushioned seat, in the shade beneath the sweet-smelling branches of the blossoming tree.

But, the next instant, there was a change. All was just as before, yet, he was One with all things. All things emanated from a common ground. All things were himself; he was all things. It lasted a moment; an eternity. Now, years later, at the brink of death, the memory of it returned. He was filled with excitement, certainty. Lying upon the dirt of the forest floor, he totally forgot his six years of agony and pain. He was absolutely sure that he had just again found the

path that led toward Enlightenment!

"Starvation and self-punishment," he thought, "have not brought me any closer to what I experienced briefly that day as a child. Now my body is weak and I will need all my strength to go on. It is senseless to punish and weaken my body so. I have reached the end of that road. It is time I took proper nourishment once again." He looked up. Before him stood Sujata, a maiden from a neighboring village. In her hands, she held a bowl of sweet milk rice. She had heard of this severe and holy hermit in the forest and had come to receive his blessing. Siddhartha accepted her timely gift and gave her his blessing with all his heart.

But his five fellow ascetic disciples were enraged. "What!" they cried aloud to each other. "Has even the ex-prince weakened?" Turning to Siddhartha, they shouted, "You are a quitter! For a little bit of food and comfort you have lost the Truth! We will never follow you again! You are no ascetic. You are just a worldly man!" And, in great disgust, they gathered their meager belongings and stormed angrily away.

Alone, then, Siddhartha ate attentively, in silence, letting his body gradually regain something of its former energy and ease. When he had finished, and at last felt strong enough to stand, he took up his ascetic's staff and slowly drew himself to his feet. Then, very slowly and carefully, but with increasing vigor and determination in every step, he made his way to the shore of the Nairanjana River, which flowed nearby.

And there he bathed. The matted filth of years washed slowly away. And with it went the last remnants of Siddhartha the ascetic. Siddhartha the awakening man grew stronger. Breathing in the fragrance of the leaves and of the rippling river air, he felt his taut nerves become steady and calm. As he watched the tiny waves slide endlessly into the shore, over and over, in perfect, translucent crescents at his feet, his senses grew unified and clear. A curtain was lifting within him; a veil was being drawn. Everything he looked upon—water, rock, sand, and sky—held incredible depth and richness; yet everything was simply itself. Still, he had not yet reached the end of his long path. The road led on.

He waded out of the river onto the shore. Taking up the now empty offering bowl, he cast it far out into the very center of the river. There the water was deep and dark and ran most swiftly. As he threw it, he called out, "If this is indeed the day of my Supreme Enlightenment, may this bowl float upstream!"

The beaten-metal bowl fell in an arc toward the river. The sun shone on it and the bowl seemed to turn to gold. The bowl hit the swirling river with a splash and began at once to forge upstream, leaping like a glistening salmon until it came to the whirlpool of Kala Nagaraja, the Black Snake King. There it whirled down into the jeweled chambers of his underwater palace, settling at last against a whole long row of identical golden bowls. The Black Naga King slowly raised his ancient, hooded head and cried, "To me, all of time is but a memory! Though it was an eon, to me it seems only yesterday that an Awakened One last arose. This day shall see the arising of another!" And then, swaying in the shimmering light, he took up his ancient songs of triumph and joy.

And the ex-prince, Siddhartha Gautama, strode like a lion towards the Bo tree. He came to it in the soft light of the late afternoon. "This is the spot," he said. "Here I shall take my stand and finish the long battle once and for all!" Heart-shaped leaves hung quietly from the sturdy branches of the tree. At the base of the trunk, the earth was smooth and even; the shade was soothing and cool.

Just then the poor grass-cutter, Sothiya, came along balancing a woven basket of the day's cuttings on his shoulder. "Noble Lord," he said, "please take this as your seat."

In his hand he held eight bundles of freshly cut grass. Then he set off again on his own way.

Then the future Buddha spread the grass on the earth at the base of the tree. He seated himself on it, folding his legs under him like the massed coils of a mighty serpent. Then he announced, "Though only my skin, sinews, and bones remain and my blood and flesh dry up and wither away, I will not move from this seat until I have attained Full Enlightenment."

And he pressed forward in his meditation once again.

Then many shimmering visions took form all around him. All the force of life's clingings to states of joy, comfort, and ease came swaying gracefully to him in the form of three beautiful women, the three daughters of Mara. "Come with us, mighty prince," they sang tenderly, as they approached. "You have triumphed like a great bull; like a great sweating bull you have finished all labor. Come, Great One! Like a mighty serpent who sheds his skin you have shed all earthly cares. Come to us, Great Hero, and you shall have your reward!" They held out their arms, danced slowly before him, and watched him slyly through painted eyes.

Siddhartha smiled at them like a man who watches puppets. The women said, as if with concern, "Take care, O man of flesh and blood. Act now or you will lose your chance for eternity with us—you will lose it forever. We are the prize of which all men really dream. Don't act the saint, you who are a hero!" But Siddhartha remained seated and unmoved. "If you fail to gain us," they now cried, stamping the ground angrily, "worse, much worse will come." Siddhartha sat silently, absorbed and still. Already they were forgotten. The shouting women grew old and withered and, with a final hoarse shriek, they vanished.

Then all life's deepest fears of death, hells, horrors, pain, ugliness, and the unknown sprang up like demons out of the gathering twilight. They took form and mobbed him, shrieking of torment and deformity, of all manner of terrible and disgusting experience. They descended upon him whirling like a flock of hunger-maddened crows who try to tear a few scraps of meat from a stone—and cannot.

Siddhartha strove on in silence. His mind grew clearer and clearer, beyond all traces of fear or desire. Then the demons—the horse-headed and red-eyed, the tiger-striped and vulture-clawed, the elephant-bellied and boar-tusked, the wielders of iron whips and burning spears, the hurlers of copper razors and adamantine discs, the blood-chillers, their screaming silenced, vanished back to their worlds of darkness and pain.

Still Siddhartha sat on steadily, silently, unmoving.

Then Mara himself, riding on his great war-elephant, "Mountain-girded," at last approached the future Buddha with a final piece of trickery. All his usual ploys had failed. In desperation he took on the habit-voice of Gautama's own thoughts and began to question him. "How can you hope to achieve this? You are just a pampered ex-prince. For a few years you've worked hard, it's true. But while you were still clinging to the skirts of the palace women, real men were out here killing themselves to reach this goal. What makes you sure you can do it? Really. Are you worthy of coming to Enlightenment today, right now? Think of it, Siddhartha, Enlightenment! Supreme Enlightenment!"

But the future Buddha only touched the earth lightly with the fingers of his right hand and asked the humble earth to witness for him.

Then the earth replied with a hundred, a thousand, a hundred thousand thousand voices: the voices of furrows and graves; the voices of youth and age, man, woman, and child; the unheeded cries of beasts; the quick, unknown, silvery language of fish; the sweet twinings of plants and the warm gray crumblings of stone. All were one voice now, thundering, "He is worthy! There is not a single spot on this

earth where, through endless lifetimes, he has not offered his own life for the welfare of others. Yes! He is indeed worthy of Supreme Enlightenment!"

And Mara, utterly beaten, fled. His sharp-tusked war-elephant bowed and left, too.

But the future Buddha only pressed on and on, swallowing up the darkness with his own light until, with the dawn, his Mind rose clear and radiant and obvious as the daybreak. And when he glanced at the Morning Star he found Enlightenment itself, crying out, "Wonder of wonders! Intrinsically, all living beings are Buddhas, perfectly endowed with wisdom and virtue!"

It was December 8th and he was thirty-five years of age. He had achieved his goal. The path to Truth had been reopened. In the steadily rising morning light, a Buddha now sat beneath the suddenly blossoming tree.

Stillson's Leap—
A Jataka

On a
cold afternoon,

late in November, a squadron of Spitfires were flying back
across the English Channel. The sky was low and gray with
few breaks in the clouds. They had just driven off a forma-
tion of enemy planes and, if their luck only held a bit longer,
all would make it back safely to the base.

But, suddenly, flames leapt from the engine of the
commanding officer's plane. The fighter shuddered, arched
over, and began hurtling down toward the sea, some six
thousand feet below.

The canopy slid back and the pilot tumbled out, away
from the flames and smoke. The others saw his parachute
open and watched him drift down through the wind and silence toward the ocean that splashed, foamed, and tilted,
yawning below. Circling above, they saw him hit the sea
and, supported by his inflated vest, swim away from the en-
tangling lines of the sinking chute. He waved them off awk-
wardly and they could not tell if he was injured or not. Despite his order, the other pilots continued to circle, waiting
for his raft to surface. But it never appeared. Perhaps the
flames had scorched it or maybe a splinter of bullet-shat-
tered metal had torn it as he jumped. In any case, without
the raft, he wouldn't have much chance of surviving in that
freezing water until the rescue launch arrived.

They radioed their position over and over, many flying now with almost empty fuel tanks. George Rothwell,

acting squadron leader, peered down through the wind-screen, and a wave of rage and helplessness, bitter as gall, swept over him. What could he do? He knew what his first order must be. And he knew he had to give it—now.

"This is Red Leader. Last circle. Form up on course."

The squadron reformed; all, that is, except one pilot. John Stillson continued circling. Once again Rothwell ordered him to reform. Stillson flew on.

"Stillson! Reform. Now! This is a final order."

Stillson's voice came back through the brittle crack-lings of the headset. "He'll never make it alone. I've worked it out. My fuel's just about gone so I'm going to ditch here. We'll share my raft. That way at least we'll each have a chance. Tell them you've got two down. See you later."

There was a loud, crackling sound; then, silence. Stillson had pulled the radio leads.

They all saw him at the far side of his turn, glinting in the sun. The fighter banked sharply, the canopy slid open and, almost instantly, Stillson dropped out, tumbling away from the warmth of the tiny cockpit.

He fell a long way, his chute blossoming like a petal behind him. Then, he, too, floated down toward the seething water which rose up beneath his dangling feet.

A mile away his empty plane plunged into the sea, kicking up a long column of spray. A rainbow hovered briefly there as the sun, for a moment, burned through the low clouds.

The others, banking instinctively, saw Stillson strike the choppy, glinting surface of the Channel; they saw him sink and then come frothing up into that brief moment of sunlight. They saw him cut loose from the shroud lines and kick free of the billowing, sinking chute. His raft inflated and they saw him pull himself in and paddle over, through the waves and freezing spray, to where the commanding officer, the CO, was still struggling in the bitterly cold water.

He hauled the CO in with him, into his own tiny raft. On their next pass, their last, the others saw both men bobbing safely in it together. Then the clouds closed in.

The others all made it back safely to the base—just barely. And waited. But no word came. In the morning, the sky was clear and they flew out over a sparkling sea. But no traces of the two men were found.

Rothwell grew unusually silent and grim. For several days, he flew out, between missions, over the sea. He watched the waves flashing by beneath his wing and saw the shadow of his plane skimming tirelessly below. He dropped down so low that he could see the bubbles spinning and bursting between the wave crests. But the sea remained empty. It scrolled out endlessly, unbroken in every direction. He gave up in bitterness.

The war ended and Rothwell found himself, more or less, in one piece. He took up a career and made plans to marry. But he had bad dreams. Sometimes skeletal aircraft, their naked ribs exposed, tore past his wing, and burning cities, glowing like cinders, slipped by below. Sometimes immense clouds massed thickly above him, burning red as blood in the eerie light of an unseen sunset. Once three silver stars glittered before him. He flew toward them through a vast, empty, deep blue sky. But they came no closer. His fuel was just about gone and only the bottomless sea splashed below when he awoke. Sometimes red tracers and white-hot cannon shells searched after his life. Despite every trick, he could not escape them. They came closer and closer. He awoke, wide-eyed, having seen men die.

What he saw most, though, was the day that Stillson and the CO had been lost. He relived it many times, as once again he saw the burning plane, the falling men, the opening parachutes, the raft bobbing below, and, finally, the clouds swirling in, obscuring all. Then he would wake, tormented and sweating, in the darkness, thinking, "All right, Stillson had leaped. It had been a noble gesture and a courageous one—but futile, failed. Where had it led in the end? Instead of losing just the CO, we lost Stillson, too—perhaps with no need. So what good was it? Who knows? Maybe he could have made it back with the rest. It had been Stillson's choice. What more could I have done anyway?" Rothwell would think on. "My job was to get them back. My orders were clear." And, once again, he would try to put it out of his mind. But it was never any good. He would have no peace. He would remember it all again.

Sometimes he found himself thinking: From where had Stillson drawn the courage to shove himself out alone like that? Men jump, after all, when they have to, when they must. But for Stillson to have leaped like that was something else. It was a mystery to him, profound and unsettling.

However, of one thing, at least, he grew sure. Despite the futility of Stillson's effort, he would probably never see a finer or braver thing in his life. Still, the terrible, seeming waste of Stillson's tragic leap rose up before him like a barrier which he could not pass. It remained part of him, a disturbance in the very flow of his blood, a psychic embolism perhaps; something from which he could not be free.

Once, as he was motoring in the country, a herd of young heifers suddenly lifted up their heads and began to run alongside his car. It was uncanny the way they ran beside him. It was as if they were responding to the turmoil still buried within him. They trailed after him, running on their own side of the rough stone fence, jostling each other and bawling loudly until they reached the stone wall that enclosed their field, and they were forced to stop. They bunched against the wall, the whites of their eyes glistening; a dark line of tears trickling across their muzzles. Their cries seemed frantic, mournful, weird, and positively unearthly. Rothwell felt it was almost as if they were trying, despite great difficulty and from across a vast distance, to

communicate, to send some kind of message. Crazy as it seemed, he swore that he could almost hear words, words saying, "We are beasts, dumb, horned creatures, mere cattle. Though we protest our fate, still what can we do? If it is our lot to be butchered by men, there is no escape. But you, you are a man. Don't let your chance slip by! Let your dark dreams go! Understand and live!" He drove on as if crazed.

One night, at winter's end, he happened to walk out to a deserted beach. A cold, salty wind blew in from the sea buffeting him as he passed from the protection of the bare trees and stood on the strip of uneven, pebbled sand. The far-off drone of a distant airplane echoed across the sky. He looked up. White stars were glittering overhead, fading and reappearing from behind high, thin, shifting clouds, Black waves broke before him in glistening foam; silvery bubbles spun, bursting and reappearing over and over again. Thoughts rose like bubbles in his mind. "Soon delicate blossoms will unfold on the branches of the trees. In the morning the sun will rise and, in time, a full moon will glow, round and yellow, in a summer sky. Stars, waves, bubbles, suns and moons, buds on trees; they all vanish and return," he thought, like dreams, just like dreams."

Suddenly he grew very calm, alert, as if poised on a precipice. His mind cleared and became bright as all bitterness fled. Then his heart leaped out into the darkness towards the stars and everything was clear. "Why, it wasn't a failure! No! Not a failure at all!"

Words formed of themselves flashing over and over within him: "No effort is wasted; nothing dies. All things are transformed and all things live forever. Noble deeds, too, are never lost. Though they may seem fruitless, they flower in the depths of time."

He turned, walked from the beach and drove home. The war was over.